SOFT WORDS BUTTER NO PARSNIPS

The life and times of
John Iliffe Poole [1888-1979]

An ordinary man who overcame all the odds
and thus became extraordinary

SOFT WORDS BUTTER NO PARSNIPS
The Life and Times of John Iliffe Poole

© Lynda Franklin 2008

First published 2008

By Wunjo Press
Hummersea Cottage
North Terrace, Loftus
North Yorkshire TS13 4JF

Printed by:
Advantage Digital Print Limited
Bridport Road, Dorchester
Dorset DT2 9FT
01305 751267

British Library Cataloguing in Publication Data. A catalogue record for this book is available from the British Library.

ISBN 0-9548778-2-9

Also published by Wunjo Press:

An Evil Boy by A H 'Witt' Wittridge
Shoestring Warrior by Lynda Franklin

www.wunjopress.com

DEDICATION

This book is dedicated to John Iliffe Poole, Winifred Ryder Stevenson Poole and their son Donald Ryder Iliffe Poole because they were not able to tell their story themselves. It was written for Barbara Iris Stevenson Poole Wittridge and Albert Howley Wittridge by one of their children for the others: Virginia and her son Beau; Donald, son Seekio and daughter Charlotte; and of course, my daughter Zoë. May it help to put a few pieces in the jigsaw that is our family. On most every page there is one of the little homilies and proverbs with which my grandparents loved to pepper their conversations and which became part of the fabric of our life together.

A brief explanation of the title "Soft Words Butter No Parsnips". This was one of my Grandfather's favourite sayings and its aptness to his lifetime struggles will become apparent as you read through this book: it means that you should judge people by what they do rather than by what they say - particularly when their words are full of platitudes and flattery.

SOFT WORDS BUTTER NO PARSNIPS

SOFT WORDS BUTTER NO PARSNIPS

PREFACE

John Iliffe Poole was my mother Barbara's father and was 'as tough as old boots', or otherwise he would not have survived. But I didn't know about all that then. The early memories I have are largely visual and auditory and very much from a young child's perspective although no less valid. The latter memories came to me via letters, notes and photos which have given me a grown up's perspective over his life, times and most important of all, allowed me access into his mind. At the time, I was too young and self-preoccupied to know what questions to ask him, but it's as though he knew I would eventually get round to sorting out his precious papers, asking the right questions to the answers he left and allowing me to speak for him.

It was after my fifth house move in as many years that I made the decision to open up and finally deal with the contents of the boxes and files that I had been carting around the countryside. Of course, I knew they contained 'Granddad's stuff' and vaguely what was inside, but the more I read on, the more convinced I was that here, right in front of me, was a story that deserved to be told, the story of an ordinary man. No different to millions of other ordinary people throughout the world and throughout the centuries who were called upon to protect their country and were somehow proud to face death in the fight for freedom. No different to millions of ordinary people who found themselves struck down by a disabling illness, or who faced penury in their everyday lives. An ordinary man who became a pioneer. Throughout his long life he battled and fought and this is the story of how an ordinary man became extraordinary and managed to survive all the odds. And there are few things more inspirational than this to other ordinary people.

Granddad had always reminisced, but the memories tended to be rather selective and repetitive – what happened in his daily life between the landmarks? Even though there seemed to be an awful lot of bits of paper, I became a bit disillusioned because it all seemed so fragmented. I stared somewhat blankly at the handfuls of photographs, many with inscriptions. I looked at the piles of yellowed, tattered and torn letters and other documents held together with rusted pins. I caressed the medals nestling in a wooden box, was bemused by some regalia including an apron and silk sash, and sifted through hundreds of brown and grimy farthing, sixpence and penny coins. There was enough information to provide the building blocks of his life, but I still needed some mortar to consolidate it all. To my rescue came the wealth of press cuttings that once I had carefully scrutinised suddenly made sense of most of it, a bit like a jigsaw puzzle when the last few pieces are put in but I do apologise if there are still some gaps.

So, then, with most of the chronology in front of me, I could prevaricate no longer. I decided to empty my mind and just write. Here then, is his story.

Lynda Franklin (née Wittridge)
North Yorkshire

Lynda, age 5

1. REVEILLE

Colours of 1st Battn KOSB

SOFT WORDS BUTTER NO PARSNIPS

Everybody knew him as Pop, or Toney, but he was christened John. A tallish, well-built, sun-tanned man, he had a bald head surrounded by a fluffy band of silver grey hair. Year on year, he always looked the same to those that watched, never younger, never older, always sprightly and busy. He didn't speak like other people, it was a funny sound that he made, a sort of whispering with plenty of gulping and rasping. It all seemed quite normal to his grandchildren, Virginia, Lynda and later Donald who, not knowing their other grandfather, thought that all Granddads sounded like that. He was so well known in the village of Newton Ferrers, Devon, that his voice was never regarded as out of place by any of the other village children either. In addition to the voice, or lack of it, he wore a bright white cotton lint square across the place where his Adam's apple was or had once been. Ga-ga was what his grandchildren called him, an alliterative name that was easy for young kids to say, although once their teenage years beckoned, they unceremoniously dumped such a cissy-sounding name in favour of the more grown-up "Granddad". So Granddad he became for the remainder of the time he had left on this earth, all fifteen years of it. "Don't be a gouk";[1] his voice is ringing with impatience, "first things first - just start it at the beginning!"

ແ⁊ແ⁊ແ⁊

Queen Victoria had already been ruling for over 50 years, the last two decades as a reluctant widow, when John Iliffe Poole made his entrance into the world on the 18th July, 1888 at Berwick-Upon-Tweed in the ancient border country, to John Charles and Elizabeth W Poole. He was their first son. As John proudly put it, he was "born into the Regiment", the King's Own Borderers, where John Senior was a Corporal in the Pay Corps, having joined up in 1883 when he was 18.

The KOB had a long and illustrious history, originally created in 1689 as a crisis measure for the defence of Edinburgh against the Jacobites. David Leslie, the Earl of Leven had been authorised by King William III to raise a regiment and he did so in the record time of two hours, having recruited 800 men 'by beat of drum' along the Royal Mile in Edinburgh who all flocked to join. Within four months they were engaged in their first skirmish at Killiecrankie in Perthshire against the Highland Stuart army under Graham of

---

[1] A cuckoo, fool

Claverhouse[2] who was killed which put paid to the rebellion. Although King James' cause had been lost in Scotland, the KOB later moved on to Ireland where it successfully fought a number of battles for King William III.

The Poole - Graham family was very much an Army one; John Senior had already seen active service in the South African (Boer) war[3], as had Elizabeth's brothers Corporal A Graham and Private W Franks. Another brother Sergeant G Graham had also seen active service at Chitral[4] on the Indian frontier during 1895 to 1897.

John Iliffe didn't turn out to be a typical 'straight-laced' Victorian, maybe he was a man very much of his time, as inventive as the 1880s turned out to be. For instance, Greenwich standard time was created, the NSPCC founded, there was the first Crufts dog show, the first formal meeting of the Football League, the first parcel post and the first postal order. Epping Forest was opened as a park, the first crematorium in England was established, the first sod laid of the Manchester Ship Canal, the Severn Tunnel and Hammersmith Bridge both completed.

However progressive all these advances were, Jack the Ripper still had not been caught and continued to prowl the streets of east London. In cricket England lost to Australia for the first time which gave rise to the Ashes, General Gordon was killed, Ned Kelly hanged. The first dinner jacket was worn in public, there was the first beauty contest, the first gramophone, the first successful car patented by Benz, the first motorcycle, the Eiffel Tower was finally completed and the Orient Express had its maiden voyage. That (debatably) glorious American institution Coca-Cola was born, the Statue of Liberty unveiled, Jesse James and Billy the Kid were shot and Geronimo was forced to surrender a few years before the Battle of Wounded Knee at the close of the decade.

The comings and goings of some of the leading lights in the 1880s also reflected a time of change; a time of pioneers, poets and performers. Disraeli, Darwin and Karl Marx all died, but Igor Sikorsky, John Logie Baird, Simon Marks, Clarence Birdseye, Marie Stopes and Sir Geoffrey de Havilland

---

[2] He was popularly known as 'Bonnie Dundee'
[3] 1899-1902
[4] 1895-1898

were all born. The arts world gained such luminaries as T S Eliot and T E Lawrence (of Arabia), Charles Chaplin, Cecil B De Mille, P G Wodehouse, Jacques Offenbach, Sam Goldwyn, Igor Stravinsky, A A Milne, Coco Chanel, Douglas Fairbanks, Harpo Marx, Al Jolson, L S Lowry, J Arthur Rank, Irving Berlin and 'war poet' Rupert Brooke but said goodbye to Edouard Manet, Frans Liszt, Robert Browning, Edward Lear, Louisa M Allcott, Victor Hugo, George Eliot and Matthew Arnold. Great men of peace and war were also born in this decade, like Lord Dowding, Harry S Truman, Montgomery of Alamein, Pandit Nehru and Joe Kennedy (founder of the dynasty), while at the end of the decade in 1889 Herr Adolf Hitler was to make his dark entrance.

Image 1

Being as he was an ordinary man, John would have been the first to consider that he had no place amongst such great and distinguished people. However, he came from a respected military family and was to spend his whole life doing his duty and doing right by others - "just get on with the story!" he would be saying now, "no time for sentiment...". John was baptised at the Parish Church in Berwick-Upon-Tweed and spent his early childhood at 22 Woolmarket, moving later to Primrose Terrace in Merchiston, thereafter to 26 West Road, Berwick. One thing is certain, the growing Poole family must have needed reasonably substantial accommodation! The 1901 census shows John Senior as age 36, Corporal in the KOSB, wife Elizabeth (née Graham) a year younger. Their children at that time were John I, Hannah T, Walter H and Harry; eight more were to follow.

With the light fading on the British Empire the United Kingdom found itself engaged in skirmishes and wars throughout its empire and protectorates. It was a time of political and social unease, certainly of poverty and deprivation, but more of that later. In the early 1960s John was to recollect that he had often stayed in Glasgow as a boy and saw gangs roaming the streets at the time of the South African War. 'Strange to say', he wrote:

... it was caused by the same reason as it is in Ulster today, religion, and if one studies these two cities one can go back to the days when people crossed over from Ireland because of hard times with large families in search of work.

The twin values of frugality and industriousness must have been drummed into the young boy, the eldest of 12, from a very early age. 'I remember the convict ship in Tweed Dock that was open to the public', he wrote, 'as boys, we used to collect jam jars to get the penny for admission''.   Such careful watching of the pennies was never to leave him. Something that also never left him was the fact that he was a dyed-in-the-wool Scot, very proud of his roots and all things Scottish.   However, his father John Charles had been English, born in Warwickshire!

After a short employment as a driller (probably an under-age one) with a Berwick agricultural implement manufacturer, Wm Elder & Sons, on 10th October 1906 John made the unsurprising step of joining his father's regiment, the King's Own Scottish Borderers as it was now called. He was examined, found fit and then proceeded 'down south' to Colchester for basic training. On 30th November he made his way as part of the 1st Battalion to Egypt and the Sudan where he was to spend four years and 66 days, from 1st December to 4th February 1911. He talked fondly about his time in Cairo and Alexandria, and General Gordon was a particular hero of his.

Image 2

From 1910 to early in 1912 John served at Delhi Fort with the KOSB detachment and was very proud to have been there to witness the coronation of His Imperial Majesty the King and Her Majesty the Queen at Durbar in 1911. He wrote on the back of this postcard, 'a

Image 3

sight never to be forgotten'.

On 5th February 1912, still with the 1st Battalion KOSB, John went into service in the East Indies for three and a half years. He used to say with a touch of pride that he was so keen to get into the army that he had falsified his birth details to join up early, but there is no evidence for this. Whilst serving in India he felt privileged and proud to have spent some time with someone who had been there at the time of the Indian Mutiny[5].

Image 4

In common with many other servicemen he was to bring back artefacts from places he was stationed, mostly wooden things and brass ornaments including peacocks, oxen, bells and ashtrays. His house became full of them and a particular treasure was a pair of delicate *papier-mâché* bon-bon dishes with the intriguing inscription 'Suffering Moses, Srinigar' in spidery ink on the underneath. Suffering Moses was not a place, it was the name of the maker and his emporium still exists today. It was a fascinating exercise to retrace, at least on paper, some of the steps that John must have taken in those early years of the new century.

Srinigar, in Kashmir, Northern India, is situated at the foot of the Himalayas and surrounded by mountains and presumably the regiment must have been quartered there at some time. John (and many others before and after him) would have crossed the small river in the road and strolled between the old main post office and a colonial building that housed Grindlays Bank. There he would have come across Suffering Moses' extraordinary shop selling *objets d'art* of *papier-mâché* and woodcarvings of walnut so extraordinary he had to make a purchase. It was run by the mysterious and highly charismatic Moses,

Image 5

---

[5] The Indian Mutiny was from 1857-1859

an old wise man, the leader of an occult religious group. Continuing a family tradition going back unknown centuries, he had been trained as a painter at the very beginning of the 20th century. None too eager to part with his best items, he would wish potential customers of his finer works to be aware of just what they had purchased. It was not unusual for him to request certain customers to leave his shop and never return, with the explanation that they did not understand art in the slightest. But why Suffering Moses? "How else could I make anything beautiful? Only by suffering. I suffer for my art. You create nothing good if you don't suffer."

Image 6

෴ ෴ ෴

The first decade of the twentieth century witnessed many firsts, from the useful to the not quite so useful: the ubiquitous paper clip, the loudspeaker, colour photography, the escalator, the vending machine, air conditioning and those necessary evils plastic and cellophane, to Christmas tree lights and neon lights, cornflakes and instant coffee and artificial silk stockings. The first helicopter was designed by a Frenchman and had a maiden flight lasting a few seconds.

The first facelift was performed in 1901, the first underwater journey by submarine took place, as did the first Tour de France and the first blood transfusion. The Dalai Lama was forced to flee Tibet when the Chinese invaded Lhasa. Einstein published the Theory of Relativity and would later propose the quantum theory. Sonar was discovered, as was the magnetic North Pole, the iconic brands of Rolls-Royce and Harley Davidson established, Sinn Fein was born, Picasso invented cubism, Bleriot flew across the English Channel in a wooden plane tied up with piano string and motion pictures were demonstrated by Thomas Edison. Father's Day was initiated and the Gideon bible made its debut.

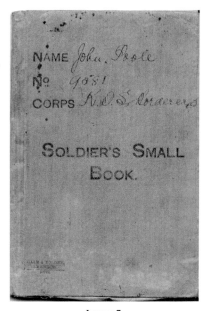

Image 7

2. PLAYING ONE'S PART

JIP in 1913

To the dozens of happy faces of John and his comrades smiling in the sunshine of India, the grim shadow of the First World War could surely have never been imagined, not even in their wildest nightmares.

Image 8

There was a 6 month spell of leave back home during the early part of 1914 although 11th August marked the official date of the end of his tour of duty in India. Then, with war looming, the 3rd KOSB made its official goodbyes to the city of Dumfries and John Iliffe Poole, along with CSM Brooks and C/Sgt Hector McKay were mentioned in a press cutting as leading the ceremony to leave the regiment's colours. John was mobilised with the 2nd Battalion KOSB in Dublin and passed fit for active service. However, instead of going straight with his unit to France, his services as an instructor were required with the Feeding Battalion of 3rd KOSB and he was promoted to Sergeant (Company A/C). As it turned out, training and advising on the successful feeding of the troops would become crucial work in such a logistically-challenged and drawn-out war.

The Poole and Graham families were well represented during the First World War. It is unclear whether Elizabeth's brothers Sergeant E Graham, Corporal A Graham and brother-in-law Private W Franks who had all fought with the KOSB in Chitral and South Africa went with the regiment to Flanders and France. However their sons Private W Graham (Highland Light

Infantry), Sergeant A Franks and Sergeant J Cape (KOSB) all saw active service.

John's youngest brother, Thomas Luke Poole[6], had enlisted in May 1914, although at the age of 16 he was already 'in camp' and wearing a uniform.

Image 9

Barely five months after enlisting he was dead, killed by a shell, age 19 during the first battle of Ypres[7] and subsequently buried at Menin Gate, Ypres. A ragged press cutting tells the stark tale:

> Private Thomas L Poole, Scots Guards, whose parents Mr and Mrs Chas Poole, West Street, Berwick, were officially informed on Sunday that he had been killed in action. He enlisted only in May and to be a soldier was his ambition. He sailed for France on October 3rd, only two days after his birthday and was killed in action between October 20th and 26th. There are few families in the British Army which can equal the record of patriotic service to which that of Mr Poole lays claim. Mr Poole himself was in the KOSB while his brother was in the Navy. Mrs Poole, who

---

[6] Pte 8947 Thomas Luke Poole, 2nd Bn Scots Guards
[7] The first battle of Ypres was from October to November 1914

was a Graham, comes of a fighting stock. Much sympathy is felt for Mr and Mrs Poole in their sad loss.

Similar words would be written some thirty years later to Mr and Mrs John Poole Jnr on the sad loss of their son Donald during the next war with Germany.

Harry Poole[8] always kept in touch with his oldest brother 'Toney' and in December 1913 sent this photograph in postcard format to John, then a Corporal in India. On the back he mentions his brother Tommy, that they were both 'real Knuts'[9]. He rushed to enlist just after war broke out.

Image 10

A year later on 18th December 1915 the family was devastated to learn that he, too, had been killed just a month before the evacuation of Gallipoli and buried at Twelve Tree Copse Cemetery in Turkey. He was twenty-one.

A man from Berwick, Mr Chas Poole, has just learned that the second of his five soldier sons has made the supreme sacrifice. A year ago his second youngest son,

---

[8] Pte 13569 Harry Poole, 1st Bn KOSB
[9] Taken to mean KOSB nuts, or fans

Pte Thos Poole, Scots Guards, was killed in action in France. On 17th December [10] his third son, Pte Harry Poole, KOSB, has been killed at the Gallipoli Peninsular. He belonged to a family which has a unique record of patriotism with 13 family members who have been in the forces.

A unique record indeed. The newspaper cutting went on to reveal that on the day before he was killed, Harry had sent a cheery letter home to his parents and in his left breast pocket they found an unposted letter addressed to his brother, John Iliffe. There was a hole clean through it which the Adjutant explained was caused by 'the fatal bullet which entered his heart'. He forwarded this letter to Mr and Mrs Poole who subsequently gave it to John. He was unutterably proud of all that this punctured and stained envelope symbolised, the letter still intact within, and he kept it close for the rest of his life as a last link with his younger brother. It was a source of wonderment to him and he was keen to show it to anyone who expressed an interest. Unfortunately, the letter was subsequently missing from his effects so it couldn't be reproduced in this book.

Many years later John was to write:

I watch the Great War series on BBC and often wonder how my dear mother felt when she had five sons in it from the beginning, plus brothers and nephews. It must have been an awful strain, seeing that two were killed and two became invalids for the remainder of their lives.

Thomas, Harry and later John were all awarded the 'Pip, Squeak and Wilfred' trio of campaign medals, ie The British War Medal 1914-1920, the Victory Medal 1914-1919 and while Harry received the 1914-1915 Star, Thomas got the 1914 Star with clasp and rose, indicating that he had served under fire.

Another brother Sergeant Graham Poole also served in the KOSB. He was badly wounded and survived the war as an invalid, but little information is available about him, apart from

Image 11

---

[10] It was, in fact, the next day, the 18th December 1915

his appearance in a few family photos of the 1930s.

Image 12

This photograph of John and a sister was taken in 1914 after John had returned from Lucknow. He was staying at 'Aunt Nettie's', Ebberston near Scarborough. John is standing on the right above one of his sisters. One sister was called Emily, another Eva and they both lived in Leeds. There is little other information about the six sisters. Were they involved in the war effort? The above articles in the press relating to the deaths of Thomas and Harry are good illustrations of the early days before the woman and her role in society assumed any sort of importance.

Of the remaining two brothers, Corporal Sandy Poole and Sergeant Walter Poole, little is known except that they fought with the RASC in the second war.

John was further promoted to Colour Sergeant in 1917 and on 19th September he was finally on his way to Flanders, via France, where as part of the 29th Division he was to get his first taste of life in the trenches.

Image 13

3. NO MAN'S LAND

Postcard, Oldest Allies in Europe

The most abiding and harrowing images of the First World War or indeed any war, must surely be the scenes of brave soldiers on both sides slugging it out in the trenches. The Germans had, in effect, got there first so they had the pick of the best strategic sites across France to build their trench fortifications on the higher ground and thus the Allies found themselves having to dig down in areas that were only a few feet above sea level. It naturally followed that two or three feet below the surface there would be water. If the trench was made of clay it soon became waterlogged, if it was excavated from sandy soil it would sooner or later collapse. Trench life thus became a never-ending fight against water and mud, with additional water seeping from big craters that guns, shells and bombs had made.

Image 14

They say an army marches on its stomach and although the British Army tried to ensure the soldiers on the Western Front, especially those in the front line, were well fed it was an uphill struggle given the logistics of this particular theatre of war. Everything that was eaten was prepared in two large vats which could then taint the taste of the tea when plain water was boiled in them. During the Great War something like 3,240,948 tons of food was sent to the soldiers in France and Belgium, cooked by 300,000 field workers for onward transmission to the men in dixies[11], petrol cans or old jam jars and was invariably cold once it reached them. The soldiers understandably became very critical of the quantity and quality of food.

---

[11] Military cooking pots or camp kettles

Eventually the Army moved the field kitchens closer to the front line but never close enough to give the men the hot food they badly needed.

At the outset of the war British soldiers were allocated 10 oz of meat and 8 oz of vegetables per day but as the size of the army grew and the German blockade became more effective, the rations had to be reduced, although the men on the front line were given fractionally more. Men would club together to buy a primus stove but couldn't always find fuel. The bulk of their diet had been bully beef[12], bread and biscuits but by 1916 flour was in such short supply bread was being made with dried, ground turnips and even then it could take up to eight days before it could get to them. There had to be a strong reliance on cans and one of the most infamous was a tinned concoction called Maconochie[13] which was described as 'edible when warmed, but a man-killer when cold'. Later, the main meal often consisted of a pea soup with a few lumps of horsemeat, and kitchen staff had to become more inventive with roadside weeds. As a slight sweetener, each division of some 20,000 men received 300 gallons of rum which was distributed after an offensive or during very cold weather. The French and Germans were more generous.

As you would expect in such conditions, disease was rife. Trench foot was an infection caused in cold, wet and unsanitary conditions from standing for hours and days in water without being able to remove footwear. The feet would gradually go numb, the skin would turn red or blue and if untreated could turn gangrenous with the only solution being to amputate. The remedy was a little idealistic and consisted of drying the feet and changing socks several times a day. What was more achievable was giving added protection by smearing the feet with whale-oil grease; ten gallons of the stuff was used every day by just one battalion.

Lice were another hazard and apart from being an irritant on the skin, they carried trench fever which accounted for about 15% of all cases of sickness in the British Army. Latrines consisted of pits four to five feet deep that were supposed to have been filled in when the level came to within a foot of the top, but there was never any time to do this and usually the men had to make do by using shell holes. Little wonder that dysentery became a

---

[12] Canned corned beef
[13] Sliced turnips and carrots in a thin soup

widespread problem, caused by the unsanitary conditions and contaminated water. Soldiers were supplied with water bottles that could only be refilled when they returned to the reserve lines, but unfortunately they didn't hold enough and the men often had to resort to gathering impure water from shell holes and other cavities. As a safeguard chloride of lime was often added to the water but soldiers disliked the taste.

Due to time restraints and other considerations, many men killed in the trenches were hastily buried almost where they fell, so when a new trench or dugout was needed large numbers of decomposing bodies would be discovered just below the surfaces. All these bodies combined with decaying food scraps would attract the unwelcome attention of rats. If one pair could potentially produce as much as 880 offspring in one year, it is not difficult to imagine that the trenches could literally be swimming with them. 'The rats were huge', wrote one soldier, 'they were so big they would eat a wounded man if he couldn't defend himself'.

Shell shock, as its name suggests, was a condition caused by continued exposure to shell fire, not surprising in view of the large quantities of shells used. For instance, during the first two weeks of the Battle of Passchendaele, the Allies fired over 4 million shells and throughout the whole of the First World War, they used a staggering 5 million tons of artillery shells. Early symptoms of this distressing illness included tiredness, irritability, giddiness, lack of concentration and headaches which would eventually result in mental breakdowns making it impossible for anyone afflicted to remain in the front line. Between 1914 and 1918 the British Army identified 80,000 men (2% of all those who saw active service) as suffering from this condition. Some sufferers were summarily executed for desertion when, in fact, they were merely disorientated and in the early stages of shell shock. Nowadays the Armed Forces recognise a less severe but still very debilitating condition called Post Traumatic Stress Disorder, PTSD.

Faced with the prospect of being killed or permanently disabled, some soldiers hoped they would receive what was known as a 'blighty wound' and be sent home. Some would deliberately shoot themselves and consequently SIW (Self Inflicted Wounds) became a capital offence. A total of 3,894 men in the British Army were convicted of this although none actually faced the firing squad and were jailed instead. Others would kill themselves rather than carry on in the trenches and the usual method of suicide was to place the muzzle of their Lee-Enfield rifle against their head and press the trigger with a bare big toe. Another way was to deliberately court the attention of a German sniper, not hard to do since he was probably only a few feet away.

If ordered to attack, the soldier would have to advance, lugging with him a total of 30kg of equipment which included rifle, 2 Mills grenades, 220 rounds of ammunition, helmet, wire cutters, field dressing, entrenching tool, greatcoat, two sandbags, rolled ground sheet, water bottle, haversack, mess tin, towel, shaving kit, extra socks, message book and iron rations. Quite a slow target for the waiting enemy, especially across the often desolate and treeless No Man's Land. Advancing into enemy territory had other drawbacks. The men were even further away from the field kitchen and as such were often forced to rely on their iron rations[14]: a can of beef, a few biscuits and a sealed tin of tea and sugar which could only be opened with the permission of an officer. These emergency rations didn't last them very long and subsequently their need for food could well force them to abandon ground they had just won.

Despite all of these difficulties, soldiers were encouraged to write letters to friends and family as keeping up morale became an essential element of this long, drawn-out war. The Defence of the Realm Act of 1914 meant that all letters had to be read and censored but some officers could not bring themselves to read their men's letters and they arrived in Britain unmarked. A total of twelve and a half million letters were sent to the Western Front every week which took only two or three days to reach their final destination. By 1918, 4,000 soldiers had been drafted in to work for the Army Postal Service.

୬୬୬

September of 1917 found John once more in the trenches, this time in France, having emerged largely unscathed from the horrors of Flanders. His fate, and thousands of others had already been sealed under Haig's master plan. An assault on Cambrai was the next objective for the 29th Division.

---

[14] Emergency rations

4. A 'HARUM-SCARUM AFFAIR'

Post card, Earl Haig

Military historians have a tendency to claim that the battle of Cambrai was a British victory - Liddell Hart called it 'one of the landmarks in the history of new warfare, the dawn of a new epoch' - but in truth it had very little impact on the strategic or tactical situation of the Great War.

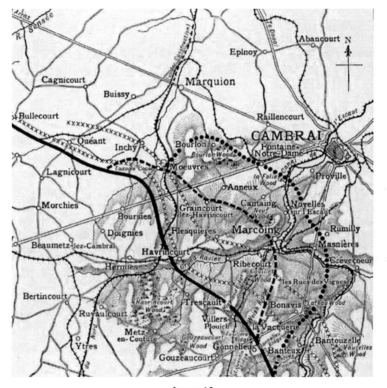

Image 15

Three months prior to the battle Sir Julian Byng[15] had consulted Earl Haig, requesting permission to make a surprise assault at Cambrai in what was considered later as a 'sketchy but audacious plan' and which, if successful, would have possibly allowed everyone to move on from the deep disappointment of Passchendaele. Cambrai was probably chosen as much

---

[15] General The Hon. Sir Julian Byng, Commander Third Army

27

because it was in Byng's area and the Tank Corps believed the ground was to their advantage as for any other sound military reason.

In order to capture Cambrai, the Hindenburg (or Siegfriedstellung) Line had to be breached. The brainchild of Hindenburg[16] and Ludendorff[17], this was an impregnable system of defensive fortification behind Germany's northern central sectors of the Western Front. Built in August 1916, it was a massive construction of trench works consisting of a series of sectors with their own system of strong points fortified with barbed wire, ditches and fire power stretching all the way from Arras to Leon.

Why Cambrai? Situated as it was in the very northernmost département of France, the Nord-Pas-de-Calais, Cambrai was once a fortified town, and although its walls had been largely ruined by the end of the 19th century, some of its gates and towers remained. After falling to the Germans in 1914, Hindenburg made it his HQ. It was an important railhead, billeting and headquarters town as it lay on the Saint-Quentin canal, at an important junction of railways on the supply routes from Germany and the northern and eastern industrial areas of occupied France, as well as a lateral route along the western front for movement of men and material. As a military target, Cambrai would be a useful capture to deny the enemy a key part of his communication system. But even if the defences could be breached, it would be difficult to fight through such an industrial town.

The battle of Cambrai was certainly a milestone in modern warfare with the first demonstration of certain sophisticated techniques and technologies including accurate survey of gun positions; mapping of enemy positions through aerial and ground observation; calculated reckoning of invisible enemy battery positions through triangulation on sources of sound and gun flash; advanced local meteorology and understanding of the effect of weather on the flight of the shell; improved reliability of munitions through improved quality control in manufacture and calibration of the wear condition of the gun barrel. In addition, success relied on the training of battery officers and NCOs in the mathematical methods required to turn this complex set of factors into physical settings of the fuze[18], sights, elevation and position.

---

[16] Paul von Hindenburg, Chief of German General Staff
[17] Deputy Chief of Staff, German 2nd Army
[18] Simple pyrotechnic detonating device

However, these new technologies were still evolving and had not yet been enthusiastically adopted; perhaps due to lingering doubts about their effectiveness.

The planned role for the tanks was to advance *en masse*, to crush wire defences and suppress firing from trenches and strong points. Using fascines[19] as makeshift bridges to cross wide trenches helped to remove one of the known shortcomings of early tank design. Much attention had been given to training, particularly for co-operation between infantry and tank. Much had been done to improve infantry confidence in the tanks, previously viewed as a mixed blessing. Another innovation was that the infantry would follow the tanks through the gaps they made, moving in 'worms' rather than the familiar lines.

A surprise bombardment using predicted firing became a key part of the Third Army's plan and a major success was that they managed to conceal an assembly of more than 1,000 guns and howitzers on the fronts of III and IV Corps. It was not just surprise that made the artillery effective: weight of firepower and the proportion devoted to neutralisation of enemy batteries were also important factors. The number of guns and the stockpile of 900,000 rounds assembled for the operation were about equivalent to those used in the preliminary bombardment to the successful attack on Vimy Ridge six months before.

But it was really the use of tanks that gave Cambrai such a landmark status. Although tanks had been first used a little over a year previously in the Somme in Autumn 1916, Cambrai was the first time they had been used in significant numbers. If the secret concentration of a large number of guns was impressive, the assembly of 476[20] Mk IV tanks possibly surpassed it. Aircraft flew up and down the area on 18th and 19th November as a ruse to mask the sound of the tanks moving up. While this and other signs of unusual activity had somewhat heightened the state of alert, it was clear that the Intelligence of the German Second Army had failed to identify the imminence and nature of the British attack.

The weather had begun to worsen and the tank corps commanders feared this could once again undermine the tank's doubtful reputation as an effective

---

[19] Rough bundles of brushwood lashed together
[20] Of which 350 were armed fighting tanks

strike weapon. So it was that the opening bombardment began, in the snow, at 6.10am on 20th November 1917, and shrouded by mist and smoke, the massed tanks supported by 6 infantry and 2 cavalry broke through with comparative ease and within hours, the enemy was forced back to Cambrai, the three trench systems of the Hindenburg Line pierced for the first time in the war. By recent Western Front standards, the Allied advance was little short of miraculous - for instance, the 62nd (2nd West Riding) Division had covered an amazing five miles from their start point, a record advance for troops in battle in the Great War. The Allies' spectacular breakthrough resulted in the ringing of church bells in Britain for the first time during the war.

Image 16

First reports said that the British initial attack broke 'deeply and quickly' into apparently impregnable defences with 'few' casualties. In fact, there were 4,000 casualties with 4,200 prisoners of war in that first attack. 180 tanks were put out of action, 65 were destroyed, 71 developed mechanical failure, 43 were ditched. Notwithstanding all that, it was still regarded as being a great and spectacular achievement, the Daily Mail called it a 'Splendid Success' and headlined on 23 November with 'Haig through the Hindenburg Line'.

Such euphoria was short-lived. Successful though the day had been, with an advance five or so miles deep into a strong system of defence in little over four hours, it was towards the late afternoon that the attack began to lose impetus and things began to go wrong, which led to dismal failure a little under two weeks later. The Third Army did not achieve its objective to push through the gap at Marcoing-Masnieres and encircle Cambrai itself and the key Bourlon ridge on the north of the battlefield remained firmly in German hands.

Byng was all for carrying on, issuing orders to continue the push into the Masnieres-Beaurevoir line to facilitate cavalry, and to finish the capture of Flesquieres and Bourlon. With few fresh troops, the element of surprise lost, the tanks weakened and the field artillery in the process of moving up, the renewed attack achieved little and late on 21 November, Byng ordered the operation to halt for consolidation but, in what was later seen as a serious command failure, Haig insisted they continue with the attack on Bourlon Wood.

The Allied tanks were few and impotent in the thick woodland of Bourlon and La Folie and behind the front, mud and snow made it impossible to move along roads which were already difficult to pass because there was insufficient stone and labour to carry out adequate running repairs. The Third Army closed down offensive operations on 27 November and units were again ordered to consolidate.

After the initial surprise and a wait for reserves, the Germans launched a successful counter attack to recover lost ground, which was a surprise to the British forces who suffered heavy losses. A victory in no small way for the German 'new' infantry'[21] and the use of Hutier[22] (stormtrooper) tactics - short artillery bombardment, heavy shells mixed with poison gas projectiles to neutralise enemy, then under creeping barrage, moving forward to infiltrate identified weak points. The German attack began at 7am on 30th November. Their advance spread across 8 miles and came within a few miles of Metz and Bourlon where they met stiffer resistance from the British and their 8 divisions of fire support who 'showed reckless determination' One group of eight British machine guns fired over 70,000 rounds in an

---

[21] Kaiserschlacht
[22] Infiltration tactics designed by General Von Hutier, one of the most successful and innovative German Generals of the 1st WW

effort to stem the German advance around Bourlon. It was the Germans' turn to suffer heavy casualties.

The British effort to hold the ridge had been impressive but the timely arrival of their tanks and nightfall facilitated the holding of some form of line. The following day the impetus of the German advance was lost, but on 3rd December continued pressure led to the German capture of la Vacquerie and withdrawal of British from east of the St Quentin Canal. The Germans had reached a line looping from the ridge there to near Marcoing. Later on 3rd December Haig ordered a retreat from Bourlon and by the 7th December 1917 British gains were all but abandoned except for a portion of the Hindenburg line elsewhere.

Initial euphoria gave way to bitter disappointment with casualties on both sides estimated at about 45,000 apiece with 11,000 German and 9,000 British taken prisoner.

As a heavy hit and run raid, Cambrai had been a failure. As a more strategic operation, it was a dismal defeat. Stories began to filter back of headlong retreat; of Generals caught in their pyjamas; of new, wonder tactics that sliced easily through the British defences. Questions were asked in the War Cabinet, and resulted rather unusually, two months later, in a court of enquiry at Hesdin. One respected commentator, a former junior officer[23], said that Cambrai was a highly speculative gamble which was inexplicable and so out of character with the rest of Haig's career. Ludendorff drily commented, 'no doubt exceedingly important strategic objects lay behind the British attack, but I have never been able to discover what they were'. It was 'a harum-scarum affair, ill-planned and feebly directed', yet it remains one of the most significant battles of the First World War.

The operational factors contributing to the British defeat were outlined very clearly in the papers assembled for the enquiry. That the German counter-attack had been a surprise was denied. Suitable defensive measures had been taken and Byng would not concede that the men were tired and had not been relieved, on the contrary he said, they were, "elated, full of fight". Byng, Haig and Smuts assigned the absence of serious resistance on the southern part of the front to a lack of training among junior officers, NCOs and men,

---

[23] Charles Carrington

but the truth was more like there was a rush to undertake the operation despite advice to the contrary. The tactically poor position and thinly held front resulting from the 20th November assault was hardly mentioned and where it was, denied. Reports also talked about the panic-inducing effect of rumours of defeat passing quickly between units and back down the lines of communication. No mention was made of the breakdown of 'all arms' fighting, nor the serious communication failures that led to the Commander of 29th Division[24] claiming that he knew nothing of the German attack before it was upon his headquarters.

The fact remains that, innovative as it was, the British assault was 'insufficiently successful'. However, what the battle did provide was a basis from which operational strengths could be identified and refined and weaknesses eliminated before the key victories at Hamel and Amiens in June and August 1918. Commencing on 8th August 1918, the British Expeditionary Force undertook a series of large scale attacks on multiple fronts in which artillery, armour, aircraft and infantry operated effectively together in 'all arms' battles.

After the failure of the 'Michael' offensive in April 1918, Germany's defence relied more than ever on the Hindenburg Line. Such was its importance to both parties that when Allied troops finally breached it in late September 1918, the German Generals returned power to Germany's civilian politicians who then subsequently began to sue for peace. The rest, as they say, is history.

___

[24] Major General Sir Henry de Beauvoir de Lisle

as near as dammit

5. BLOWN SKY HIGH

British troops on the attack

John had witnessed and survived the tenuous victory of the early Allied thrust, but with each passing day he must have felt more vulnerable. It was ten days later, on 30th November 1917 during the fierce retaliation of the Germans that his luck finally ran out. Hit by an exploding shell, he was severely wounded near Marcoing to the west of Cambrai, sustaining shrapnel and gun shot wounds to his left thigh, back and buttock, right arm and scalp and part of his left heel was blown off. He had a clear memory of lying there while gas shells were 'coming over', and he 'got some of the gas' into his lungs. It would seem he was too wounded to have been able to defend himself by putting on his gas mask, that is, if he had one.

Image 17

Poisonous gasses had been around for a long time before the First World War but military officers were reluctant to use them as they were considered an uncivilised weapon and their use had actually been banned in the Hague Conventions of 1899 and 1907. The French, in the first month of the war, were the first to use them, firing tear-gas grenades at the Germans.

In October 1914 the Germans began firing shrapnel shells whose steel balls had been treated with a chemical irritant and they 'advanced' to using chlorine gas cylinders in April 1915 against the French Army at Ypres who noticed yellow-green clouds drifting slowly towards them with a distinctive smell rather like a mixture of pineapple and pepper. However, they thought it was just the enemy dispensing a smoke screen prior to an attack and orders were given for an armed attack. Once the gas reached them, the front-trench soldiers began to complain about pains in the chest and a burning sensation in the throat. Once they realised they were being gassed, the soldiers away ran as fast as they could, which created a four-mile gap in the Allied lines. Naturally, the Germans were reluctant to move forward because of the chlorine and this delay enabled Canadian and British troops to retake the position, although the Germans eventually burst through the gap the chlorine gas had created. Chlorine gas was very unpleasant in that it destroyed the respiratory organs of its victims and led to a slow death by asphyxiation.

Image 18

The right weather conditions were important for those launching a gas attack, as if the wind was blowing the wrong way, it could result in an 'own goal' and the floating cloud could easily swamp their own troops. Which is exactly what happened when the British Army launched a gas attack on 25th September 1915. By 1916 the British had produced gas shells for use with heavy artillery that increased the range and helped to safeguard their own troops.

Protection was a rudimentary affair as soldiers were initially supplied with masks of cotton pads to be soaked with urine (the ammonia neutralised the chlorine), held over the nose and throat. Others preferred to use handkerchiefs, a sock or flannel body-belt dampened with a solution of bicarbonate of soda and tied across the nose and mouth until the gas passed over. However, it was difficult to fight like this and by July 1915 soldiers were given efficient gas masks and anti-asphyxiation respirators.

Image 19

From a purely warfare point of view, one disadvantage for the side that launched the chlorine gas attack was that it made the victim cough and thus limited his intake. Both sides subsequently discovered that phosgene was more effective and only a small amount was needed to make it impossible for the soldier to continue fighting, leading to death within 48 hours. Advancing armies also used a mixture of chlorine and phosgene[25].

The most lethal and most effective of all the poisonous chemicals was mustard gas[26], first used by the Germans in September 1917 which they called Yellow Cross. It varied between being almost odourless and having a smell similar to garlic or horseradish. It could be colourless or have a light yellow brown hue. It took about twelve hours to take effect and so powerful that only small amounts had to be added to high explosive shells to be effective. It wasn't intended as a killing agent, and given its power, it was only lethal in about 1% of cases - only becoming so if the soldier was exposed to high doses. The objective was to merely harass and disable the enemy and pollute the battlefield. Once in the environment it would cause sickness for days, once in the soil, it remained active for several weeks, and once on a soldier's clothing and equipment it would pollute anyone with whom he came into contact.

Counter-measures were ineffective since a soldier wearing a gas mask was not protected from absorption through the skin, causing huge blisters and burns. If high concentrations were inhaled, it would cause bleeding and blistering within the respiratory system, damaging the mucous membrane and resulting in pulmonary oedema. Blisters over more than 50% of the body would usually have been fatal. Soldiers suffering from the after-effects of large doses of mustard gas would usually have to be strapped to their beds and it would take an agonising four or five weeks for them to die.

> I wish those people who talk about going on with this war whatever it costs could see the soldiers suffering from mustard gas poisoning. Great mustard-coloured blisters, blind eyes, all sticky and stuck together, always fighting for breath, with voices a mere whisper, saying that their throats are closing and they know they will choke.[27]

Although the use of poison gas could sometimes result in a brief tactical advantage, it was responsible for 1.2m 'non-fatal' casualties and 91,000 deaths on both sides and seems to have had no significant effect on the course of

---

[25] Called White Star
[26] Also called Yperite by the French and HS - Hun Stuff by the British
[27] Comment by writer Vera Brittain, then a nurse

the war. The Russian army suffered more than any other while British casualties from chlorine gas were 1,976 deaths with 164,457 'non-fatal', while mustard gas caused 4,086 deaths with 16,526 'non fatal' casualties.

It is difficult to ascertain which particular gas John was exposed to as he lay there waiting for the stretcher-bearers to come. Mustard gas, with its carcinogenic properties, would be the most likely culprit, but unless he was very well covered up, it would not explain why his body was not affected by the characteristic blisters and burns.

Advancing troops were not allowed to stop and care for wounded soldiers so John would have had to just lay where he fell, knowing he was in for a long wait. He would have carried with him an emergency field dressing but his wounds were too extensive for him to try and treat. Some wounded might try to drag themselves into a shell-hole for protection but this could result more often than not in them sinking into the mud and drowning. Stretcher bearers were in short supply, being usually only four per company.

Image 20

In good conditions two men could carry a wounded man on a stretcher, after heavy rain it took four men, and during that last week it had been snowing. The stretcher-bearers not only had the problem of dragging their feet out of the mud after each step, they also had to try not to rock the stretcher because the pain of shattered bone ends grating together was so intense that the wounded man was likely to die of shock. To steady themselves they would have to put out a hand which, more often than not, would come to rest on the blackened face of a half-buried, dead soldier.

We know that the 37th Field Ambulance took John to the 48th Casualty Clearing Station where he remained for a few days before being moved to the 3rd Stationary Hospital at Rouen, a journey of some 200km distant, where his back was immediately operated on. On 5th December John joined the other wounded on HMS St George where, with the aid of cocaine a 'foreign body' was removed. Once safely back on English soil, he was taken to Chester War Hospital where the severe and by now diseased shrapnel wounds on left buttock and right hand were dealt with. He was given 500 units of anti-tetanus serum, Fusol dressings on his buttock and boracic unguent on his finger.

Image 21

He was already mentioning irritation in his throat and a sore head but nothing was done for the throat. According to the medical notes he was 'improving quickly'. Perhaps not that quickly, as on 3rd January 1918 he was transferred to Roseneath Auxiliary Hospital in Wrexham where his back was 'opened up and scraped' and 'necrosed[28] bone removed'. By 16th March John was pronounced 'healed'.

How he had managed to get a 'G.S.W., back', a gun shot wound on the back, is a bit confusing since various later medical reports transposed this to 'shrapnel wounds left buttock', and 'gun shot wound left thigh'. The largest area of damage was the wound on the left buttock (just below his waist, near his spine). The shell had left an imploded scar set deep into the fatty area which looked like one of the buttons of a deeply upholstered chesterfield, and this looked the same until the day he died.

One thing is certain; the Scottish battalions were made of strong stuff, and they would never have turned their back on the enemy. They had a history of being brave and ferocious in battle, none more so than one of John's KOSB contemporaries, Sergeant-Piper Daniel Laidlaw of the 7th Battalion, who won a VC in 1915 for playing his pipes to lead the battalion into action,

---

[28] Dead bone tissue

inspiring his comrades to charge. The sound of the pipes on the battlefield would herald the arrival of "The Jocks" - warlike men often in swirling kilts which usually struck terror in the heart of the enemy. In this instance, the enemy did their best to silence Piper Laidlaw who only stopped playing after being hit for the second time. He did, however, live to tell the tale.

However, an undated press cutting amongst John's papers gave rather a sad twist to Piper Laidlaw's story; unemployed, and with a family of six to support, he was earnestly seeking employment "of any kind".

SCOTS V.C.'s APPEAL

Man With Family of Six Wants Work

A Berwick-on-Tweed V.C., Piper Laidlaw, wants work. He has been unemployed for the past two years, and appeals for a job of any kind suitable to his age (53) and condition. Mr. Laidlaw has a family of six, whose ages range from six to 22. He won the V.C. by playing the bagpipes to rally his company of the King's Own Scottish Borderers on September 25, 1915, when the men were demoralised by a gas attack.

Image 22

William Henry Grimbaldeston VC, was another famous KOSB veteran of the First World War. John had kept many press cuttings relating to CQMS Grimbaldeston, including the signed photograph (below) so it may have been that they had been friends. Like John, he was a Quarter Master Sergeant, and in September 1917 he captured a German blockhouse single-handedly at Langemarke, France.

The citation continued:

The extraordinary courage and boldness of CQMS Grimbaldeston resulted in his capturing 36 prisoners, six machine guns and one trench mortar, and enabled the whole line to continue its advance.

He was awarded the Croix de Guerre, and the Coronation Medal in 1953.

Image 23

6. WAS IT ALL WORTH IT?

Aftermath at Passchendaele

Like so many soldiers who had returned home after active service at the end of the Great War they would have needed the support of family and friends while their minds and bodies began the long road back to recovery. John must have gone through a period of readjustment and perhaps suffered the common guilt pattern that despite appalling injuries he had been 'spared' while others, including two of his own, perished.

The precise number of people killed in the Great War is not known. Estimates vary from 8.5 to 12 million but accurate measurement is impossible due to circumstances like the collapse of government bureaucracies in Russia, Germany, Austria-Hungary and Turkey. Also, governments tended to publish figures for men who were killed during military action and soldiers who died slowly from their wounds, gas poisoning or disease did not always figure in the statistics.

Most soldiers were killed during major offensives. For instance, over 21,300 were killed on the first day of the Somme and over 50% of those who took part in the attack were wounded. Loos and Passchendaele were high casualty battles. As can be imagined, being in the front-line trenches was extremely dangerous; and it has been estimated that a third of all casualties on the Western Front were killed or wounded while in the trenches.

Civilian deaths, bomb victims, merchant seamen and passengers on torpedoed ships were usually recorded, but the hidden casualties of war - those killed by disease or war deprivation were not. It is believed that about 500,000 German civilians died as a result of food shortages. Russia, again, came off worse with high civilian deaths around the 2 million mark, Serbia had 650,000 and Rumania the same as Germany (500,000).

The Influenza pandemic, which some commentators feel should also be included as a war statistic, was responsible for a staggering 70 million deaths.

Our four-legged friends also figured high on the casualty lists. At the outset of war in 1914 the British Army only owned a total of 80 motor vehicles so they quickly became reliant on the horse which, unfortunately, was destined to become yet another innocent casualty. Half a million horses owned by the British Army were killed. Mules became prized for their amazing stamina in appalling conditions, being much tougher than horses so the Army imported a huge quantity from the USA. So much so that by the end of the war, the British Army was left with a surplus of some 213,300 mules.

ಌಌಌ

Wilfred Edward Salter Owen was born on 18th March 1893 and regarded by many as the leading poet of the First World War. His shocking, realistic war poetry on the horrors of trench and gas warfare was in stark contrast to both the public perception of war at the time and the patriotic verse exemplified by other war poets such as Rupert Brooke.

Image 24

Although he had previously regarded himself as a pacifist, during the latter part of 1914 to early 1915 Owen became increasingly aware of the magnitude of the war. He enlisted in October 1915, receiving his commission to the Manchester Regiment as a 2nd Lieutenant and went to France in January, 1917. He began to write poetry about his experiences which he sent back regularly to his mother, Susan. In his first action he and his men held a flooded dug-out in no-man's land for fifty hours whilst under heavy bombardment. In March he was injured with concussion but returned to the front-line in April. In the summer of 1917 Owen was badly concussed at the Somme after a shell landed just two yards away. After several days in a bomb crater with the mangled corpse of a fellow officer, he was diagnosed as suffering from shell-shock[29].

He was evacuated to England and on June 26th he arrived at Craiglockhart War Hospital near Edinburgh. While convalescing he wrote many of the poems for which he is justifiably famous. He returned to France in August 1918 and was awarded the Military Cross for bravery at Amiens, but was killed on the 4th November 1918 while attempting to lead his men across the Sambre Canal at Ors. The news of his death reached his parents on November 11th 1918, Armistice Day, paradoxically the very day the bells rang out in England to signal the end of the war.

---

[29] Neurasthenia

SOFT WORDS BUTTER NO PARSNIPS

The Last Laugh

'Oh! Jesus Christ! I'm hit', he said; and died.
Whether he vainly cursed or prayed indeed,
The Bullets chirped-In vain, vain, vain!
Machine-guns chuckled, -Tut-tut! Tut-tut!
And the Big Gun guffawed.

Another sighed,-'O Mother, -Mother, -Dad!'
Then smiled at nothing, childlike, being dead.
And the lofty Shrapnel-cloud
Leisurely gestured, -Fool!
And the splinters spat, and tittered.

'My Love!' one moaned. Love-languid seemed his mood,
Till slowly lowered, his whole faced kissed the mud.
And the Bayonets' long teeth grinned;
Rabbles of Shells hooted and groaned;
And the Gas hissed.[30]

ৡৡৡ

It was obvious that such a war on this scale would cost dear in terms of impact on England's once-buoyant economy and could take years to repair. While the fathers and sons had been away fighting, the women filled their shoes and by 1916, there were some 2m more women in the workplace. Overseas, Britain's monopoly position had been dealt a severe blow. The leading statesmen representing the victors of World War One drew up the Treaty of Versailles which was signed on 28th June 1919, effectively concluding the end of the war. It was said that the League of Nations was founded while Europe apparently 'lay starving'. The British Government had been busy suppressing the revolts of the colonial people; the Amritsar massacre in India, deporting and jailing Egyptian nationalists and there was Anglo-Irish bitterness with the introduction of the Black and Tans.

The pre-War period of prosperity and social peace was succeeded by a period of social conflicts, lock-outs and strikes, including the police strikes of 1918-1919. In 1919 actions were taken by British miners, railwaymen,

---

[30] Wilfred Owen to his mother Susan

dockers, engineers and textile workers for higher wages and shorter hours. On the Clyde the Government became so alarmed that the Riot Act had to be read out.

In the decade from 1910 to 1920, the first aerial dogfight took place in 1914 and the first aeroplane was used to drop bombs in Belgium[31]. The Boeing aircraft company was founded, we were given the world's first commercial airline and the first parachute jump was made from an aeroplane. The German car company BMW was founded. Stainless steel, zip fasteners, Pyrex and the wireless telephone were invented, also Edison's telephone recording device. The cancer microbe was identified, as was the value of vitamins. Manufacture began of processed cheese, and Coca-cola launched its trademark curvaceous bottle.

There was the first traffic lights, the first air mail service, the first fortune cookies, the first food mixer, the first neon advertising sign was displayed in Paris[32], the first self-service food store, the first Hollywood studios were built and Charlie Chaplin was signed up for the first million dollar movie contract. John D Rockefeller became the first billionaire. American President Woodrow Wilson declared Mother's Day a national holiday in 1914. Lenin led the Russian revolution and the British royal family changed its German name to the more user-friendly, anglicised one of Windsor. The Republic of China was founded, the Ottoman period ended when Turkey surrendered to Serbia and Bulgaria and the Titanic hit an iceberg and sank.

ഏ ഏ ഏ

In February 1919 John was re-examined and 'found fit' for the army, although still suffering from throat problems, difficulties with breathing and an occasional sore head. However, it seems to have been a reasonably content period for him as he was accepted back 'into the fold':

> *I arrived at Lochend after the first world war as a senior NCO to assist with others to re-establish the regiment which was scattered. Eventually we did. It was a happy time for all of us as we visited various places and enjoyed the company of our fellow Scots. Carnegie Baths in Dunfermline, also Pittencrieff*

---

[31] In 1917
[32] Advertising Cinzano

Park were a blessing after the previous year of rough life. We used to go and dig sheep from the snow drifts, also off to Edinburgh on Saturday, Hibernians v Hearts, in company with miners from Lumphinnans which seemed to be one long street. Hope it is a lot more pleasant in this day and age of social welfare. [33]

Image 25

John continued to be plagued by a huskiness in his voice which, as a 'mild smoker', he continued to put this down to cigarettes, but the irritation was getting worse.

On extension of his service in 5th September 1920 he was examined by a Medical Board and, puzzling for him perhaps, found fit.

The big scar on his back had 'soundly healed' and they stated that 'disablement therefore is nil'.

---

[33] In Fife-shire

7. WEDDING BELLS AND WARNING BELLS

Wedding of JIP and Winifred, 1921

The regiment made its way from Dunfermline to Raglan Barracks in Devonport for a two year tour of duty and it was here that Quarter Master Sergeant Poole met Winifred Ryder Stevenson, whose parents Robert Ryder Stevenson[34] and Amelia Ellen Stevenson[35] and the rest of their family lived in an ancient Devon farmhouse called Higher Widey, its many acres spread around the Crownhill area of Plymouth.

Image 26

In the 1901 census, Robert Ryder's profession was a baker and address given as Beaumont Bakery, St Budeaux. At that time there were five children, Esther (8), George (5), Ethel (4), Ada (2) and Win(n)ifred (7 months), with Ernest Brown who was a boarder. On retirement Robert Ryder Jnr became a full-time farmer.

Winifred's grandfather Robert Ryder Senior was born in Newton Ferrers in 1821 and the 1861 census reveals that he, too, was a baker and grocer with a shop in the Plympton St Mary area. He was then aged 40 and married to Emma, 28. There were two children then, Sarah and Philip (3) and one domestic servant.

He also shows up on the 1841, 1851 and 1871 census but by 1901 Robert Ryder Stevenson Sr was a widower aged 80, living in 'Vill New Ferrers Cottage' with daughter Amelia N (27), son-in-law William Squire, and baby son Hubert W S Squire (1). There was also a Margaret Rider (sic) Stevenson who was contemporary with Robert Jr - possibly his sister,

Image 27

---

[34] born 1865
[35] born 1872

having been born in 1863 in nearby Revelstoke, and who was living in Newton Ferrers in 1881.

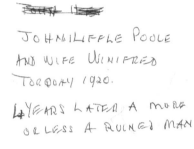

JOHN LIFFLE POOLE
AND WIFE WINIFRED
TORQUAY 1920.

4 YEARS LATER A MORE
OR LESS A RUINED MAN

Image 28

Winifred was born on 4th August 1900 and therefore only 20 when they married at Eggbuckland Parish Church in Devon on 1st June 1921. Curiously, the marriage certificate states the groom's age as 29, but in fact, he was four years older than that! They made their home in married quarters at Granby Barracks.

Image 29

Winifred seems to have been one of the lucky ones. The social impact of the Great War had been very profound. A huge black hole had been punched in a whole generation of young men as three-quarters-of-a-million British soldiers had been wiped out and roughly the same amount left incapacitated. A knock-on effect was that prospects for young women were dismal with an estimated one out of ten young ladies that could ever hope to find someone to fall in love with, marry, raise a family and lead a normal life:

> The war left behind it a generation of Eves in an Adamless Eden ... starving for love, deprived of homes and denied the joys of motherhood, many women found in friendship, one with another, some sort of substitute for these normal but lost relationships.[36]

Unlike male homosexuality, lesbianism was not illegal and a bill in 1921 to outlaw it failed because MPs considered it was wiser to sweep the whole issue under the carpet. In fact, long term statistics revealed 35% of women failed to marry during their 'reproductive' years. These ladies became known as The Surplus Two Million. The 1921 census revealed that for those between 25 and 29, there were 1,209 single women for every 1,000 men and the 1931 census showed that 50% of those women were still single.

Civil unrest continued in Britain as it headed inexorably towards a financial depression which started to bite by the middle of 1920. Trade Union membership had risen from 4 million in 1914 to 6.5 million in 1918 and 8.34 million by 1920. The Government had announced its intention to end war-time control of the mines and the mine owners subsequently demanded wage cuts. The miners unilaterally decided to strike. By early 1921 the recession had developed into a full-scale slump with the number of unemployed rising to an unprecedented 1m. In the ensuing skirmish, the Government invoked the despised Emergency Powers Act, reservists were called up, machine guns posted at pit heads and troops in battle order were drafted into large industrial areas.

The price of a gallon of petrol dropped from 4/3d to 3/5d, a tin of condensed milk was a relatively expensive 1/3d. A male clerical worker earned just less than £3 per week and a woman would expect to get about half of that.

The miners struggled on alone until June 1921 when, driven by hunger and exhaustion, they were forced back to work with their wages slashed and at the close of 1921, wage cuts had been imposed on 6 million workers. The

---

[36] Author Sybil Neville-Rolfe, *Sex in Social Life*, 1949

crying over spilt milk

effect of the recession and a feeling that the Trade Unions had somehow betrayed them accounted for 3 million workers letting their membership lapse. By mid 1922 unemployment had risen to 1.5 million - 13.5% of the insured population. There was worse to come.

ھەھەھ

Image 30

John's hoarseness was increasing; he still had no idea just how ill he was, but that would not have dampened the excitement and pride he must have felt when he was notified that, on 4th July 1921 at a specially called meeting of the Council of the Borough of Berwick-Upon-Tweed, it had been 'unanimously agreed' to confer upon him the Honorary Freedom of Berwick-Upon-Tweed in recognition of 'Eminent Services rendered during the Great War'. Judging from the signs of wear on his powder blue leather regalia, he had been at some time an active member of the ancient order of Freemasons[37], but towards later life there is no evidence of regular attendance.

On the 5th July 1921 there was the escort ceremony of the KOSB colours at Devonport church before the 2nd Battalion left for the increasingly unstable danger zone of Ireland.

---

[37] St David's Lodge No 393, Berwick-Upon-Tweed

I remember it well as I was on parade in Raglan Barracks. I was a Colour Sergeant and paraded with the Colours for the first time since 1914. It was surely a day to remember. All was still as the grave and it made lots of people think, including myself.

Away from the industrial heartlands, John must have felt reasonably at home in Devonport which he considered 'a nice, welcome place', but he was obviously mindful of the plight of his fellow man across the country. However, with a keen sense of history and an abiding affection for the places he had visited, he would have been deeply interested in the news that Howard Carter had discovered the tomb of Tutankhamen. Also, being a humanist, he would have felt it timely that Marie Stopes had opened the first birth control clinic in Britain but he would certainly not have been in the queue to buy the recently published D H Lawrence, rather racy novel Women in Love, "one has to draw the line somewhere", he would say.

However, amid all the gloom there was some very welcome news at home for John and Winfred, as just over a year after they got married, on 11th June 1922 their only son Donald Iliffe Ryder Poole was born.

In addition to the continual hoarseness, John was alarmed to find himself experiencing shortness of breath as 1923 approached and the Regiment moved back up to Redford Barracks in faraway, chilly Edinburgh. It was here that his daughter Barbara Iris Stevenson Poole was born on 28th October 1923.

Stanley Baldwin became Prime Minister and his government spent £50m on 'unemployment relief'. Woman's Hour was broadcast for the

Image 31

first time, and had John wanted to type his memoirs, a Remington typewriter would have cost him the princely sum of £26.

John's voice had become so bad that he could no longer ignore his condition and was subsequently referred to throat specialist Dr Fraser at the Royal Infirmary in Edinburgh.

Image 32

The medical record stated:

> The patient is fairly well nourished, has a very husky voice and irritable cough with slight dyspnoea especially when asleep, large swelling of the left arytenoids and false chord.

It was really quite fortuitous that he was referred to Dr Douglas Guthrie MD, FRCSEd[38], who at the time was a captain in the RAMC and Surgeon-In-Charge at the Military Hospital, Edinburgh Castle. Douglas James Guthrie was quite a remarkable man and having graduated in medicine from the University of Edinburgh in 1907 he became a pioneer in the field of ENT. After service in the First World War he became consultant Ear, Nose and Throat surgeon to the Royal Edinburgh Hospital for Sick Children, with a particular interest in speech disorders in childhood. After he retired he pursued a related interest as a historian of medicine, and one of his publications was A History of Medicine. In 1948 he founded the Scottish

---

[38] 1885-1975

Society of the History of Medicine. John and he were men of similar age and who were to keep in touch with each other until Dr Guthrie's death.

A low tracheotomy was performed and a portion of growth sent for examination. Blood was also taken for a Wassermann Reaction Test[39] and although this turned out to be negative, none of the other tests were hopeful. Pathological examination found a malignant epithelioma, so on 21st June 1924 at Edinburgh Castle, Dr Guthrie performed a 3¾ hr operation for the removal of the larynx along with infected glands, left lobe of the thyroid, the left aryteno-epiglottidean fold and the epiglottis.

Edinburgh Castle from Johnstone Terrace.
X Window from which infant King James
was lowered in a basket

Image 33

When the larynx was removed, John's windpipe would have been severed and a hole cut into his neck to which the severed windpipe was attached. As there was now no connection between the mouth or nose and the lungs, he had to learn to breathe, cough, sneeze and 'blow his nose' through the opening in the neck. He could theoretically do anything he was able to do before the operation, except swim. To be able to talk would, hopefully,

---

[39] The standard test for TB, Malaria, Syphilis etc developed by August Paul von Wassermann

follow but he didn't know for sure whether he would be able to work out an effective technique. His lungs could no longer expel air into the mouth, so his mouth and nose were useless from this point of view. To move to a warmer climate would have been advisable because cold air would be taken directly into his lungs through the hole and could no longer be filtered and warmed through the nose. The bib was not as effective a filter as the nose had been.

He was one of the first to have this pioneering operation and later, he would refer to himself as a 'guinea pig'. Although it was recorded that the patient 'stood it well' his weight was below 9½st and he was given just six months to live.

For the following months, John was, to all intents and purposes, dumb and, without a voice box, completely and frustratingly unable to communicate. In fact, there was a matter-of-fact reference to him as 'a mute' which, although strictly correct at that time, sounded rather harsh. He wrote later that he used to find it difficult to swallow even a teaspoon of water. He was completely alone, without any supporting network and that probably accounted for his indefatigable efforts in later years trying to set up and get awareness, support and funding for laryngectomees. Much later he was to muse:

> There is so much fear, so much dread connected with it. And after an operation and the necessary after-care, patients are left very much to their own resources. I could have huddled over the fireside all my life, I suppose.

There was no-one around to teach him the rudiments of speech and as he was not one to sit back and accept his lot, he set about finding a way of using trapped air in the throat chamber to mimic sound. He must have applied himself to the task logically and diligently because he was to write, 'it was very hard work at first but once I overcame the initial difficulties the words seem to come much easier'.

The Invaliding Board must have thought so, too: 'He can talk in a whisper and once accustomed one can understand what he says. He still has a tube into his trachea'. His condition was described as 'fair' and his weight was a less skeletal 9st 11lbs. The Board findings were that he had 80% disablement due to carcinoma larynx, origin 'unknown'.

8. PENSIONED OFF

KOSB discharge, character reference form, 1924

SOFT WORDS BUTTER NO PARSNIPS

At the age of 36 when some men consider they are in the prime of their life, John was discharged from his beloved regiment on 24th October 1924 as being 'permanently unfit for further service on account of war wounds and after-effects of gas'. But he was to find out that this simple sentence did not mean that his employers, the Army, War Office, Ministry of Defence, the Government or whoever, would accept any liability for his condition, far from it.

He had served in the King's Own Scottish Borderers, man and boy for 18 years and 15 days and would soon receive the Long Service and Good Conduct medal to be added to the 'Pip, Squeak and Wilfred' campaign medals awarded to him just after the war. Prompt payment of his standard pension arrears backdated to April was sent to him the very next day, although an amount was subtracted as already forwarded by the Regimental Paymaster. He had to re-apply to the Royal Hospital Chelsea for continuance of this service pension award. Luckily, a few years earlier John had become a member of the Prudential Society because at that time there was no general provision for unemployment or healthcare.

FOR ALL CLASSES
OF
INSURANCE
CONSULT
THE MAN FROM
THE
PRUDENTIAL

Image 34

John was to receive four references, two dated seven months before his operation, just as though he was, typically, getting his affairs in order and anticipating either that he would die during the operation or soon afterwards or that he would be discharged. Barely four months later he was obviously trying hard to find employment, and despite the following selection of glowing endorsements he was never to take paid employment again, either with the Army or in 'civvy street':

> He has always been a thoroughly reliable and honest soldier ... very efficient with initiative and tact and in his handling of men and working with officers ... very temperate and a good disciplinarian ... thoroughly trustworthy and efficient ... in every way a man above the average always willing to help or do any work ... particularly good at Company accounts ... steady and hard working ... an excellent Quarter-Master Sergeant most suitable for any position of trust ... has a good education and is conscientious and industrious.

A letter dated 7th November 1924 from the Captain Adjutant, I KOSB at Redford Barracks, Colinton, would probably have forewarned him of this:

> It is regretted that no suitable vacancy for Mr Poole exists at present … in the event of a suitable vacancy occurring in the future …

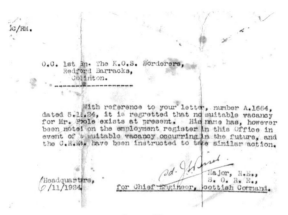

Image 35

One wonders whether he would ever have been lucky enough to find work even if the job market had not been quite so bad as, in those early days because of his unusual voice he may have been considered a bit of a freak. In the months following John and Winifred would have been preoccupied making the long move down south to warmer climes, but he still managed to write a few letters as he was still waiting to hear from either the Royal Hospital, Chelsea or the Ministry of Pensions.

John wrote reflectively:

> *I can still see the pipes and drums playing retreat every week, also the brass band every Sunday, church parade, and pipes and drums taking the Scots to church. Little did I think when I left for the depot as a healthy man playing football, cricket and hockey, that in 1924 I was to return more or less an invalid, in a hope that in a warmer climate I would survive.*

Finally at the close of 1924 came the news he had hoped would not come. The Ministry of Pensions pronounced that 'the disability from which you are suffering', carcinoma of the larynx, was 'neither caused or aggravated by your Great War service in the Army'.

Image 36

In real terms this meant that they had decided not to grant him any 'pension gratuity or allowance'. The accompanying form stated that any appeal must be lodged 'within 12 months'.

Dr Guthrie was 'very surprised' at such a decision:

> Personally I have no doubt about the matter, you had suffered from hoarseness since being gassed in 1917, and I feel sure that this irritation was the cause of the tumour growth. I should certainly advise you to appeal against the decision and if I can be of any service, I shall be very glad. Meanwhile you may make use of this letter as you please.

So in January 1925 although the battle had been won, John's fight was far from over. A lifetime member of the local Conservative and Unionist Association, he solicited their help and immediately the local MP, Major Kenyon-Slaney stepped in to intervene, writing immediately to the Ministry of Pensions requesting that:

> ... some disability pension in addition to his 18 years service pension may be obtained for Mr Poole who was invalided out of the KOSB's on account of carcinoma of the larynx.

The reply was that it was 'admissible' for Mr Poole to appeal as he was discharged prior to the termination of the war 'which for official purposes was 30th September 1921'.

John subsequently applied to the Royal Hospital, Chelsea giving notice that he intended to appeal. The appropriate forms were sent out, he confirmed he had received them, he filled them in and sent them off, he confirmed they were sent off, the Royal Hospital confirmed they had received them and forwarded the claim to the Minister of Pensions, and stated that a decision in respect of eligibility for disablement pension be notified direct.

Meanwhile, another notification came regarding his service award. The Royal Hospital had 'reviewed the case' and awarded a pension of 25/9d a week backdated from 25th October 1924 in lieu of service award. This was to increase by 5d at age 55, and 4d a week from age 65, and subject to 'good character as a pensioner'.

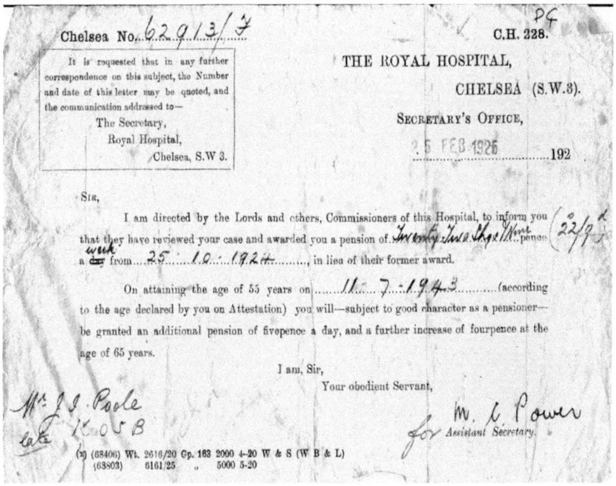

Chelsea No. 62913/7 PG C.H. 228.

It is requested that in any further correspondence on this subject, the Number and date of this letter may be quoted, and the communication addressed to—
The Secretary,
Royal Hospital,
Chelsea, S.W 3.

THE ROYAL HOSPITAL,
CHELSEA (S.W.3).
SECRETARY'S OFFICE,
25 FEB 1925 192

SIR,

I am directed by the Lords and others, Commissioners of this Hospital, to inform you that they have reviewed your case and awarded you a pension of Twenty Two Shgs Nine pence (22/9) a ~~day~~ week from 25 . 10 . 1924, in lieu of their former award.

On attaining the age of 55 years on 11 . 7 . 1943 (according to the age declared by you on Attestation) you will—subject to good character as a pensioner—be granted an additional pension of fivepence a day, and a further increase of fourpence at the age of 65 years.

I am, Sir,
Your obedient Servant,
for M. C. Power
Assistant Secretary.

Mr J. J. Poole
late KOSB

(68406) Wt. 2616/20 Gp. 163 2000 4-20 W & S (W B & L)
(63803) 6161/25 „ 5000 5-20

Image 37

Two months later a letter came backdating pension arrears from 15th April 1925 to 13th October 1925 to 32/-, plus 14/- for wife and child but was subject to deduction of Award notified 14th August 1925 of £2/6s.

But it is extremely difficult to work out the exact picture from all these impersonal, faded pieces of paper that served as letters, but quoting from the more important ones here in this book seemed valid.

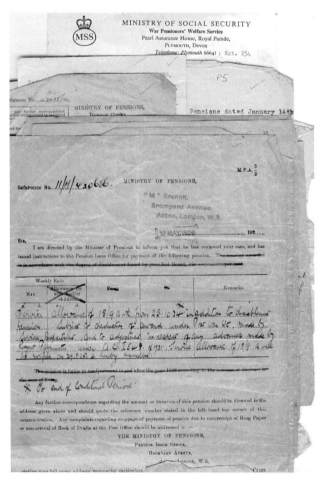

Image 38

Each letter that arrived was obviously hugely important to John, both in terms of his mental state and its relevance to how well his family would survive. They would often take the form of a standard matrix with handwriting in the blank spaces. How did John manage to interpret such apparently random official communications? Were they intended to bemuse and confuse?

He was obviously eligible for the standard service allowance for himself for over 18 years service, and at the outset he had been declared 80% disabled, although the main cause of this was still not considered due to war service. There was also an award for 'wife and child' even though he had two young ones. It was also interesting that the goalposts seemed to fluctuate; it seemed that such dispensation was almost at the whim of whoever was dealing with the case at the time. In John's terms, he had been prepared to give his life up for the Army and his country, and nearly did, and one can feel the sense of deep disappointment and loss as he tried to reconcile the impact of one after the other of these brief sentences. That he felt let down must have been an understatement and it's hard not to think that the powers-that-be, having used men like John as cannon fodder, now wanted to sweep all the aftermath under the carpet.

One thing was certain, John and most of his contemporaries would never have willingly gone 'cap in hand' to ask for handouts. He felt he had earned this 'pay' and was in the invidious position of having a young family to support and he could not work because of his disability. There was a 'double whammy' here as he had been paying for years into the Prudential and somehow he was not getting back what he had expected from them either.

In May 1925 the Pensions Appeal Tribunal became involved. Over a month later Mr Smale, MP, asked the local Plymouth Ministry of Pensions to investigate, and a day later John arrived for an interview. A follow-up letter confirmed their suggestion to him to lodge a claim for a pension and a further letter received from the Ministry of Pensions enclosed the necessary forms to claim a pension under Article 9 of the Royal Warrant in respect of 'G.S.W. back'[40]. Rather confusingly, it went on to request an employer's certificate 'shewing state of health has interfered with employment' and

---

[40] 'Gun shot wound, back'

rather curiously asked him not to mention the Carcinoma of Larynx 'in respect of which appeal has been made to Pensions Appeal Tribunal'.

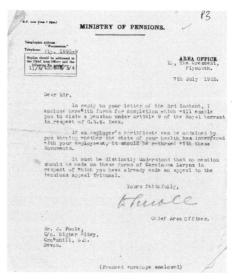

Image 39

On 8th July 1925 the pension award was backdated to this date of 40/- pw plus allowance for child 14/- until 7th December 1926, total £3/4s. However, it was conditionally 'in addition to Service Allowance and subject to deduction of all former awards from 8th July 1925'.

The Ministry of Pensions wrote that it was sending to the Pensions Entitlement Appeal Tribunal statements regarding the grounds of the case and the decision he was appealing against. In preparation for this, the Ministry's own statement ran into nine thorough pages and concluded:

> During service the appellant was wounded in the buttock and scalp also in the foot and was gassed, all the same date. In view of the history and the absence of any supporting evidence to connect the condition with service in the Great War, the Ministry is of the opinion that the trouble is of post-war origin and cannot be accepted as either due to or aggravated by War Service.

John's signed statement was poignant but typically to the point:

> *My parents are alive and well, there is no sign of my disease among any of my parents' relatives. To me, this points that my disability arose through the inhaling of gas[41] in November 1917. My head annoys me, at times also my back, no doubt as I get older I shall feel it worse. The winter is beginning to cause me a bit of annoyance. Now I am completely disabled my voice is completely gone with no hopes of its return, also I find it hard to breathe at times, that impedes me from doing any manual labour. I have applied for different situations but cannot fulfil their requirements through my disability. I have a wife and two children aged 1 and 3 to provide for and see to their future.*

Attached to this was an open letter from Dr Douglas Guthrie, certifying that John Poole, formerly Quarter-Master Sergeant, was well known to him as he had removed his larynx for malignant disease a year before. He said that John had previously been hoarse since he was 'gassed on active service in 1917', and he had 'no hesitation at all in attributing the disease to the irritation of the gas'. He added that John had been seen before the operation by Sir James Dundas-Grant of London, who shared Dr Guthrie's opinion regarding the cause.

This letter may well have tipped the balance of the scales because, after a very long nine months, on 30th July 1925 the Pensions Appeal Tribunal finally gave its final decision: the carcinoma was 'attributable to service in the Great War'. But what about the pension for the gun shot wound in the back?

At the end of August John received a further letter saying that his case had been further considered and a revised service allowance award has been made of 18/9d per week but this time, no allowance for wife and/or children. This was in addition to the Disablement Pension <u>and</u> subject to cancellation of award by Service Department from 15th April 1925. John obviously queried the make-up of this award as the Ministry confirmed receipt of a further letter.

On 18 September a money order was enclosed for arrears due in respect of revised award from 15th April 1925 to 1st September 1925. John asked about

---

[41] He would refer to it rather casually afterwards as a 'dose of gas'

the next medical board sitting, he also applied for arrears. On 9th October he received a money order in respect of arrears of £17/10s for wife and child's allowance from 15th April 1925 to 6th October 1925. On 7th October a further money order was enclosed for wife and child's allowance from 7th October 1925 to 13th October 1925 at 14/-.

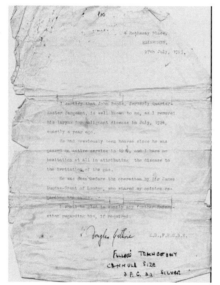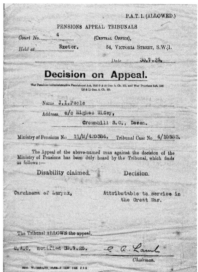

Image 40

The Ministry wrote that they would be continuing the pension at the same rate while arrangements were made for him to attend a further examination by the Medical Board. He eventually received a reply to his request for arrears:

> … as you allowed 4 months to elapse after being notified of the Ministry's decision before you lodged your appeal to the Pensions Appeal Tribunal, it is regretted that arrears of pension prior to 15th April 1925 cannot be granted.

The Medical Board sat again on 4th December, but John had to wait a further three weeks for their decision that a revised disability award of 40/- weekly rate (man), allowance for child 14/- from 8th July 1925 to 7th December 1926. In fact, the same amount as he was given months previously. Another

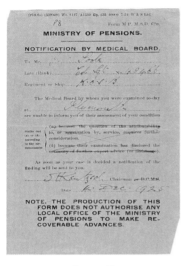

Image 41

medical examination was due in two months to enable 'further consideration' of his claim.

Two weeks into the new year, there was a disappointing reply to John's request regarding allowances for his wife and children. He was not eligible to receive any family allowances in respect of 'disability gunshot wound back', as his marriage took place after the date on which he sustained this disability. Furthermore, 'the regulations' did not

Image 42

permit any allowance being paid in respect of Barbara Iris, as she was born 'more than 280 days after the date of the official termination of the war'.

John subsequently visited the Ministry of Pensions in Plymouth, bringing with him all information regarding the Tribunal where he made another claim for arrears. Letters go back and forth, one in particular of 27th April explained that his case was under 'special consideration' and the documents were returned on 18th May 1926.

ও৯৯৯

The economy and fabric of industrial Britain was moving towards a dismal conclusion: the General Strike of 1926 which became known as the most bitter and significant struggle in the history of the British working class. A year before 'the workers' had planned the formation of a new industrial alliance composed of miners, railwaymen, transport workers and engineers who had correctly anticipated that when their one year agreement with the coal owners came to an end in July 1925, an unprecedented crisis was bound to ensue. In March 1925 the miners had met the coal owners, the latter demanded wage reductions and longer hours, the miners refused to yield, the owners gave notice terminating the existing agreement, proposing wage cuts and refusing to recognise the principle of a minimum wage.

There had been Black Friday, and Red Friday and now it was all-out battle which began on 3rd May 1926. At its zenith, approximately five million workers took strike action in solidarity with the miners. Who could not have had sympathy with them as the mine owners repeatedly cut their wages? Between 1922 and 1924 alone 597,198 miners were injured at work. On average, one miner was killed every five hours, and 850 suffered injury every day. Miners' pay varied from region to region and in Lancashire, for instance, their reward was just nine shillings a day.

Industry was at a standstill and many newspapers stopped printing. The Government's strike-breaking machinery leapt into action. All naval and military leave was cancelled, troops were moved to London and industrial centres, infantry marched through Liverpool with steel helmets, rifles and full equipment. The battleships Ramillies and Barham were recalled from the Atlantic fleet and anchored in the Mersey. Warships were anchored on the Tyne, the Clyde, the Humber and at Bristol, Cardiff, Swansea, Barrow, Middlesbrough and Harwich. The military infiltrated the strikers, there were baton charges by armed soldiers. Nine days later the leaders of the trades unions declared unconditional surrender while the miners struggled on for a further six months but by October 1926 hardship had forced them to capitulate, alone and defeated. Many were victimized and remained unemployed while the ones that were accepted back were forced to accept longer hours for lower wages. The final humiliation came in 1927 when the Government passed the Trade Disputes and Trade Union Act which, amongst other things, made all sympathetic strikes illegal.

9. PEACEFUL WATERS FLOW

Postcard, Newton Ferrers in 1925

SOFT WORDS BUTTER NO PARSNIPS

In between May and June 1926 John and Winifred moved to Glen Cottage, Riverside Road, Newton Ferrers.

Image 43

They had been living for the last two years at Widey Farm with the in-laws, and it was there that he got into his lifetime routine of rising at 5am to help with the farm chores. Although still weakened by his ordeal, susceptible to the cold and damp and prone to breathlessness, he must still have managed to work enough to satisfy himself that the slate was always clean between him and his father-in-law. For the rest of his life he was to ensure that he "never owed nobody nowt".

As Winifred's grandfather John Senior had lived and died in Newton Ferrers, it is not beyond the realms of possibility that the little cottage was inherited by Winifred, or maybe it was a bequest which served as a late wedding present. Four years after their move John was to become steward of the reading room, and with it came a tied cottage adjoining Glen Cottage.

In the mid 1920s Newton Ferrers and Noss Mayo were unspoiled chocolate box villages that faced each other across the Yealm estuary - the shortest river in Devon rising ten miles away in Dartmoor. Plymouth was five miles by sea and about 11 miles by road, in those days a rather alarming circuitous route. Both were essentially little fishing villages and were linked at low tide by 'the voss', a brick-lined causeway, and at other times by little ferry boat which would row or scull visitors and locals across the creek for a couple of pence. Cars would have to travel around past Bridgend at the head of the creek.

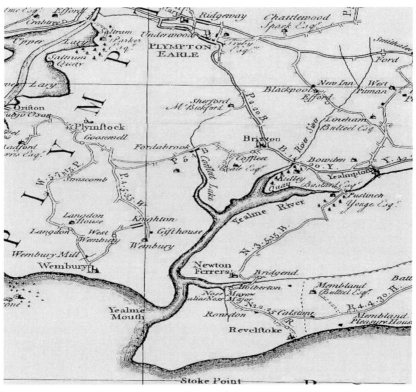

Image 44

In 1850 William White[42] described Newton Ferrers as 'a pleasant scattered village, on rising ground, at the head of a small creek'. The population of the parish was then 778 and it extended to 2,991 acres. There were nine farmers, one blacksmith, a corn miller, a boat builder, cider dealer, two RN pursers, a land surveyor, one ferry and fisherman, a thatcher, an auctioneer, four boot and shoe makers, three carpenters, eight coal dealers, two masons, four shopkeepers, two tailors and two carriers who went to Plymouth three days a week. Well known local surnames were Foster, Hodge, Hosford, Carter, West, Roach, Hockaday, Tope, Crocker, Doddridge, Kingcombe. The only public house was the Dolphin Inn supposedly named after the shoals of dolphins that frequented the estuary. There was a Victorian reading room and village school dating from 1874, post office, village stores and the buttery which as its name suggests sold milk and all manner of dairy produce, and later a Co-operative store.

Image 45

Holy Cross Church, Newton Ferrers had been founded in 1084 and had one of the oldest foundations in Devon but the present-day church structure dates from the 12th -14th centuries having been extensively remodelled in the 1880s. Accessed through an old oak lych gate, the church and its windswept graveyard had a commanding view of its twin St Peters across the river at Noss Mayo.

Mr White mentions the oyster beds 'belonging to companies in London and Southampton' and that a variety of other fishing was carried out. In fact, Newton had developed as a fishing community, dating back untold centuries.

---

[42] History, Gazetteer and Directory of Devonshire, 1850

Even up to the first World War there was still a fleet of some 27 sturdy crabbing boats, 'greybacks', but by the time of the second World War this trade had declined dramatically. The fishermen were justifiably proud of their skill under sail as unusually the estuary faced into the prevailing winds which, with the right conditions, developed a tidal bore which pushed waves right up the Newton creek a mile or more in from the sea. The local name for this phenomenon was 'the Sitch'. "'Tis sitching badly" was a phrase heard in bad weather and completely unique to the Yealm estuary and bore a striking resemblance to the French word 'syche', meaning 'bore'. Probably borrowed from the French fishermen who came there to use the baulking stores[43] built by Lord Revelstoke.

Between 1878 and 1927 there were three lifeboats but surprisingly they were only called upon four times in fifty years. The annual Regatta was an important event and apart from the sailing, swimming and sculling, the greyback race between Newton and Noss was one of the most anticipated events all year. It apparently pre-dated the more celebrated Oxford and Cambridge boat race but unfortunately ended around the time of the second World War.

With its mild climate and picturesque setting Newton Ferrers began to gain quite a reputation as a beauty spot and a Mr James Ford from Plymouth was not slow in realising its potential. In the late 1890s he began to develop the area, starting with the Yealm Hotel, complemented in no small way by the opening of the railway line to Yealmpton in 1898. With its sheltered creeks and deep 'pool' Newton was becoming a haven for yachtsmen too, and a favourite way for the more wealthy to holiday in the mid-war years was to have a houseboat moored on the river. At the turn

Image 46

---

[43] For handling and packing catches

of the century steam boats and paddle steamers laden with inquisitive visitors would travel the 45 minute journey from Plymouth on day trips to sample local hospitality and to admire the views but by the late 1920s coal had become very expensive and these boats were gradually withdrawn from service.

In 1932 the Council for the Preservation of Rural England commissioned a survey of the area[44] and this was their brief assessment:

> These two villages, secreted on opposite sides of a winding creek off the Yealm, have become better known since the frequent bus service was established to Plymouth. Only a few of the inhabitants still carry on the occupation of their forefathers as fishermen, but most of the cottages from the seventeenth and eighteenth centuries have survived and the grey slate and thatch roofs of the older cottages give to the place an atmosphere something akin to the best of the Cornish fishing villages. The valley above the Newton creek is serene and unspoilt, and the small village green near the old church forms an attractive approach from Yealmpton.

However, even then there was a note of concern:

> There is a considerable amount of building land for sale with commanding views of the river; but anything built in this conspicuous position will seriously affect the landscape unless of harmonious colour. The woodlands which clothe the banks of the Yealm are essential to the beauty of this river and it would be of great advantage therefore, if the landowners on both sides could cooperate in preventing any increase in the number of temporary structures that have been erected in the woods above the Coastguard Station.

Also there is a charming quote from a book written in the mid 1930s[45]:

> Noss Mayo creek is very interesting, if only because of the keen rivalry and separatism between Noss on one side of the creek and Newton on the other, said to be due to the former being a Celtic settlement and the latter Anglo-Saxon. Be that as it may, they are at present similar in being villages with more boatmen to the square yard than you will find anywhere along this coast. Every cottage seems to have its own landing stage and the boats' painters pass in even through the

---

[44] The author was Mr W Harding Thompson
[45] *Under Sail Through South Devon & Dartmoor*, Ray Cattell

bedroom windows, presumably being tied to the bedstead or the toe of some sleeping yachtsman. Except for one or two mouldering stone ruins and a pretty group of houses by the ferry, there is practically nothing to interrupt the soft sweep of the wooded hills which flank the whole of the tidal Yealm and its creeks upstream. It is a scene wholly natural and sweet. One can see above the woods the far grey tors of Dartmoor.

Image 47

Although money was extremely tight, Donald and Barbara had, by all accounts, the most marvellous childhood in the most jewel-like of settings.

They had two caring parents and the love and support of the extended Stevenson family network. Both children attended the village school and had lots of young playmates.

Barbara had fond memories of visiting her grandparents' farm and riding cows like horses, without saddles of course! Winifred was an excellent horse-woman.

Image 48

money doesn't grow on trees

Image 49

It must have been a sad time when her father eventually sold Higher Widey in the 1930s so the council could build row upon row of much-needed housing. A contemporary press cutting explains what secrets it gave up just prior to demolition. Nowadays it would probably be Grade 1 listed and saved for the nation.

LINKS WITH PAST AT PLYMOUTH FARMHOUSE

LINKS with the past have been uncovered at the 300-year-old farmhouse at Higher Widey Farm, Widey Lane, Crownhill, Plymouth, which is soon to be demolished. Mr. J. Barber, assistant curator of Plymouth City Museum, has carefully examined the farmhouse.

One of the most spectacular discoveries in the house was a granite fireplace, measuring 6ft. 6in. across, 3ft. deep into the wall and 5ft. high. The fireplace had been blocked-up and hidden by bricks, stones and debris. Similarly obscured and adjacent was an interesting oven used for bread baking. It was 2ft. 3in. in diameter with a domed roof 2ft. high. It was heated with sticks, which were raked out when the oven was hot enough to put the dough inside. Mr. Barber even found some charred sticks still in the oven.

The date of the house was determined by the main oak staircase with its massive turned balusters, and confirmation of the date came from the mouldings on a window frame which, when uncovered from the plaster, matched the staircase. There is a second staircase, which is spiral and recessed into a wall.

The 2ft.-thick walls are made of "shillet"—a local name for slate —and the floor is stone.

A large 13-foot-long oak beam was found in the roof which was carved along one side and had obviously been used in another building with the carving exposed. It had been used in the roof structure of Higher Widey Farm and was covered with plaster.

Mr. Barber said: "One of the things that makes the house interesting is that it signifies the tail end of the Tudor and Jacobean style." It was typical of its period with its thick walls, massive, finely carved staircase, huge chimney stack, and large rooms.

Image 50

10. THE TURBULENT TWENTIES AND THREATENING THIRTIES

King Kong movie poster, 1933

SOFT WORDS BUTTER NO PARSNIPS

On 3rd June 1926 John travelled to London, where he was 'an exhibit'[46] at a symposium called Sections of Laryngology. This expedition would have cost him the majority of his week's pension, and to get to Wimpole Street from the train station he would have taken one of those new-fangled red double-decker buses that had just entered service.

Douglas Guthrie MD presented his paper: 'A Patient who underwent Total Laryngectomy two Years ago and has since acquired a useful Voice'[47]. John spoke from the podium and also separately to throat surgeons. Dr W Morrison, a learned American surgeon was present. He went on to study John's method of speaking, details of which he took back to America with him. In time his adapted version of John's method was introduced back to England and used as a blueprint to facilitate speaking in lieu of a voice box. Taking coals to Newcastle? Some years later in 1934 the Daily Mail was to cover a story about the good doctor's work.

Back to money matters. On 8th June a payable order was received including arrears from 25th October 1924 to 14th April 1925 and from 8th July 1925 to 12th January 1926. On 28th September 1926 his case was again reviewed and John was again awarded 32/- pw, with 14/- allowance for wife and child from 15th April 1925 to 13th October 1925.

On 22nd November the case was once again reviewed:

> I have to inform you that the Award notified to you on the attached form viz that your disablement has been assessed at one hundred percent for life in respect of Carcinoma of Larynx and G.S.W. Back and is hereby declared to be the final award. In accordance with that award a pension for life has been granted to you in accordance with the degree of disablement found by your last Board, viz 100%. Man 40/-, wife and children 14/- (whilst eligible). From 8th December 1926 for life. In addition to service allowance. Rank for pension: Private. Remarks: Wife and child eligible in respect of carcinoma of larynx only. This amount is liable to adjustment if at any time after March 1929 the rates of pension or allowance should be varied in accordance with the cost of living.

Why should his rank for pension be a Private when he had been a Sergeant? The language and content were quite baffling. Anyway, he fought on, finally

---

[46] The Royal Society of Medicine, Section of Laryngology, Summer Meeting
[47] Their random capital letters

receiving a letter from the Ministry of pensions on 7th January 1927 which went some way to explain this anomaly:

With reference to your recent enquiry respecting payment of rank and child's allowance, your case has been referred to Ministry HQ and I have to inform you that you are not entitled to rank allowance as you are in receipt of a service allowance which includes allowance for rank and you are only entitled to disablement pension at Class V rates. With reference to an allowance in respect of your child Barbara Iris, an allowance is not payable as she was born more than 280 days after the dated of the official termination of the Great War.

Image 51

This was the last full communication from the Ministry of Pensions. So, with his pension now at the full rate of 100% disability, John received a total of £2/14s or 54s for a wife and two small children. Seen in context, the minimum wage for a footballer was by then £8 per week while a baker earned on average 64/4 per week and a bricklayer's labourer 54/1d. A cabinet maker in London earned an average 73/6d and one in Birmingham earned 8s less. Wages for the miners had been cut right down, but a ton of coal was well over £1 to buy. A cine camera cost £16, a straw hat stitched with gold thread 3gns (£3/3s), the same as a gramophone record while a lightweight raincoat cost £1/4s, a Viyella nightie 17/11d, a girl's school dress £1/9/9d, a manicure 1/6d, a bottle of Johnnie Walker Red Label whisky would set you back 12/6d, a pint of beer 5d, and a jar of marmalade 7½d. Shredded wheat cost 1/10d a pack, a tin of Colman's mustard was 2/1d, a tin of Heinz tomato soup cost 9d. Curiously, a one pound tub of lard cost 8d in Liverpool and 1/- in Ipswich! A bishop earned £2,000 pa and an immigration officer (male) would earn between £200 and £300 pa. The cheapest cinema ticket would have been 9d with a Manchester to London return train ticket costing £2/6s, just a little bit more than a gold bracelet watch at £1/9/6d.

SOFT WORDS BUTTER NO PARSNIPS

The mid to late 1920s had got off to a flying start. Charles Lindbergh flew non-stop across the Atlantic in Spirit of St Louis; Amy Johnson flew solo from England to Australia; on Pendine Sands Malcolm Campbell set a new world land-speed record in Bluebird at more than 174mph.

Women finally got the vote; the Morris Minor was launched, the first Elastoplast made; £1 and 10s notes came into circulation. John Logie Baird demonstrated the 'televisor', the spin-drier was launched, Mickey Mouse made his debut in Steamboat Willie; Al Capone and Bugsy Malone fought it out in the St Valentine's Day Massacre; Ramsay MacDonald cautiously appointed the first female cabinet member. Wall Street crashed, as did the R101 airship in France killing 48 people. The draft Highway Code was issued, the YHA formed and, nothing new, there was an outbreak of foot and mouth disease.

ৡৡৡ

With the matter of his pension now finally put to rest, all seems to have gone quiet, except for a slight contretemps over a boundary between John and a neighbour resulting in a warning letter from David Foot Nash, Solicitor:

> You yesterday assaulted my client in the most violent manner and it was only by good fortune that he escaped your onslaught.

Image 52

Oh dear! Some months later there was another incident. John received a Summons to appear at the Court House, Yealmpton to answer charges that he did 'unlawfully assault and beat' Cecil Henry Daymond contrary to the Offences Against the Person Act 1861. No further information is known. These actions seem quite at odds with anyone that knew John and with the description of him on at

Image 53

least two of his references as being a 'very temperate' man!

On 6th February 1931 John contacted the Prudential requesting his case to be put in front of the committee. As usual, it was a matter of principle. He didn't want special treatment, just clarification and justice as he had tried to explain that he couldn't obtain any satisfaction and was not able to get in touch with someone there who could make a decision.

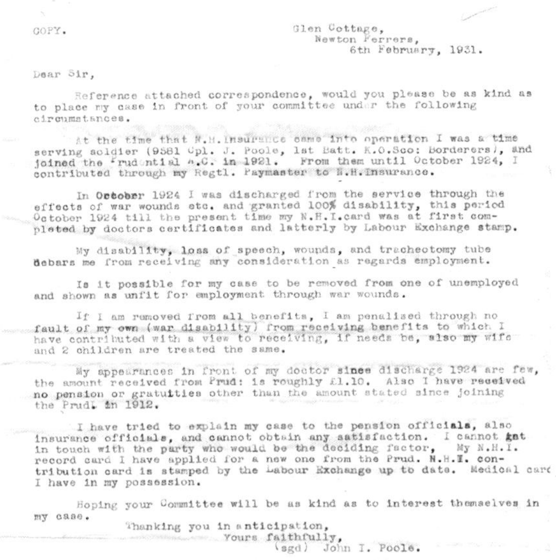

COPY.

Glen Cottage,
Newton Ferrers,
6th February, 1931.

Dear Sir,

Reference attached correspondence, would you please be as kind as to place my case in front of your committee under the following circumstances.

At the time that N.H.Insurance came into operation I was a time serving soldier (9581 Cpl. J. Poole, 1st Batt. K.O.Sco: Borderers), and joined the Prudential a.C. in 1921. From them until October 1924, I contributed through my Regtl. Paymaster to N.H.Insurance.

In October 1924 I was discharged from the service through the effects of war wounds etc. and granted 100% disability, this period October 1924 till the present time my N.H.I.card was at first completed by doctors certificates and latterly by Labour Exchange stamp.

My disability, loss of speech, wounds, and tracheotomy tube debars me from receiving any consideration as regards employment.

Is it possible for my case to be removed from one of unemployed and shown as unfit for employment through war wounds.

If I am removed from all benefits, I am penalised through no fault of my own (war disability) from receiving benefits to which I have contributed with a view to receiving, if needs be, also my wife and 2 children are treated the same.

My appearances in front of my doctor since discharge 1924 are few, the amount received from Prud: is roughly £1.10. Also I have received no pension or gratuities other than the amount stated since joining the Prud. in 1912.

I have tried to explain my case to the pension officials, also insurance officials, and cannot obtain any satisfaction. I cannot get in touch with the party who would be the deciding factor. My N.H.I. record card I have applied for a new one from the Prud. N.H.I. contribution card is stamped by the Labour Exchange up to date. Medical card I have in my possession.

Hoping your Committee will be as kind as to interest themselves in my case.

Thanking you in anticipation,
Yours faithfully,
(sgd) John I. Poole.

Image 54

He explained that he had joined the Association in 1921 and at the time the National Health Insurance came into operation he was a serving soldier. His NHI contribution card was stamped up to date 'by doctor's certificates and latterly by Labour Exchange stamp'. John wrote that his disability, loss of speech, wounds and tracheotomy tube debarred him from receiving any consideration for employment and he, quite simply, asked for his case to be removed from one of 'unemployed' to one of 'disabled' as he had contributed for many years and now needed some financial help.

He wanted his card returned so that it could be stamped and he confirmed that he received no benefits from the Labour Exchange. Confined to bed with a cold for 2 weeks, he wrote again to the Prudential on 3rd March 1931 because they hadn't answered any of his questions and if no decision could be given, to whom could he apply? 'Is there no committee where cases like this can be investigated verbally instead of by letter which is not always entirely clear?' he asked.

The corresponding copy form stated:

> Insurance prolonged till 31st December 1929, extended till 31st December 1930, specially extended till 31st December 1931. Member states he is unfit for employment owing to war wounds and received no consideration regarding employment. He desires to know whether he could be treated as unfit for employment owing to war wounds instead of unemployed. Should case be dealt with as a transfer to Navy, Army and Air Force Fund for invalided men or shall we inform member that he will be entitled to medical help up to 31st December 1931?

Although there may have been some extra pennies involved, it certainly would not have been his main concern. How humiliating for such a man to have been labelled as 'unemployed'; 'unfit for work due to disablement from war wounds' would have been far more accurate and appropriate.

John obviously kept himself busy, but how different it would have to have been in paid employment, after all, he was still only 43 years old. Providing for his family was his main concern, and although they had to 'make do and mend', they seemed to lack for nothing. But the right responses must have eventually been received from the Prudential and for the next seven years he

Image 55

managed through thrift and good household management to "keep the wolf from the door".

♥♥♥

The early to mid 1930s were again very unsettled. The New York Stock Exchange had crashed in 1929, resulting some two years later in a worldwide depression.   Unemployment in Britain had been rising steadily and had reached three million - one in four of the workforce - and the Jarrow March attempted to highlight this. Churchill was trying to persuade the government of the seriousness of Adolf Hitler's intentions, and even the TUC was calling for a boycott of Germany in protest at Hitler's rise to power following the Night of the Long Knives in 1934 and a year later Nazi Germany staged the Olympics.   The Spanish Civil War began in 1936 and the VW Beetle was introduced to a waiting world.

There was the first car radio, pick-up truck and electric kettle. Crystal Palace burned down, Egypt allowed Britain to use the Suez Canal for 20 years, Bonnie and Clyde were captured, George V died, Edward VIII never took over, which left the stammering and unprepared George VI to eventually ascend to the British throne. On a brighter front, England won the Ashes, Fred Perry became the first Briton to win the US Open Tennis championship, the film King Kong was released, Monopoly went on sale and the Potato Marketing Board dreamed up the Eat a Potato campaign because we apparently weren't eating enough of them.

♥♥♥

Five years on from the meeting John attended at the Royal Society of Medicine, the Mail got hold of a Big News story from New York: a man without a voice box had broadcast over the radio! The article gave an interesting insight into the method John used when he had taught himself to speak "without no help from nobody" and it is therefore worth reproducing the whole of the article:

> Those who have been made speechless by the removal of their larynx need no longer despair. Though they cannot breathe air through the nose and mouth but must do so through a silver tube in the neck they can be taught to speak with other organs and, strange as it may seem, largely by the aid of the gullet. Recently a man without a voice box broadcast over the radio. The feat created tremendous interest.

When, however, I called upon the man's teacher, Dr W Morrison, to enquire as to the present condition of this supposedly very unusual case he disclosed that a number of ex-patients who have lost their larynx are now going about their daily business in a normal manner. Dr Morrison said:

> One advantage of the method of making these mutes talk is that there are no mechanical contrivances to get out of order. I do not operate in these cases. I simply teach people a way to talk. I did not originate the method, it was first used in Europe[48]. I have perhaps made some improvements in technique.
>
> The problem of teaching a person without a larynx to speak is quite a complicated one. Because the patient is without vocal chords, we must find some part of his throat where something can be made to vibrate. We must also find something to act as a bellows to blow air past the new vocal chords. Remember, the patient no longer breathes through his nose and mouth. The task is to supply not only a new vocal chord apparatus but also an air reservoir. This reservoir consists of the deepest part of the throat itself and the tube leading from the throat to the stomach, called the gullet or oesophagus, and perhaps to some extent the stomach itself. The gullet is meant for the passage of food. It does not contain much air under ordinary circumstances, but it can be made to play the part of the lungs.
>
> I teach the mute patient to swallow air deeply into the throat. I make him gulp a big mouthful of air into the gullet, just as if he took a mouthful of food or water, and swallow. With practice, a patient can learn to bring up this air from the gullet, and even from the stomach, and with it to make a noise in the throat. The air bellows now working, we must look for something to act as vocal chords. Fortunately in the deep part of the throat there is something that can be made to vibrate. The patient now progresses by practice and further exercises to learn to change the first rough, low-pitched sound of the air coming from his gullet into syllables and words which can be clearly heard.
>
> When he can do this he as achieved the possession of a power of speech without a voice box. With continued practice, the production of the new voice becomes easier for him, louder, clearer and more easily understood. Finally he will do it almost without thinking of what he is doing at all. He will be able to do everything but sing. A stranger would notice little wrong - some hoarseness, perhaps, and rather a monotonous sing-song voice. How long does it take to learn all this? That depends on the patient. If the man is intelligent, eager and

---

[48] By a certain Mr J I Poole!

willing to make the effort required to find out how it is done, it is only a matter of weeks.

John scrawled on the bottom of the article that he had been an exhibit at the Royal Society of Medicine on Thursday June 3rd 1926, two years after being made a laryngectomee. He wrote that 'this American surgeon' had studied his method, improved upon it and it was brought back to Britain. 'Now it is used all over', he wrote rather understatedly.

At this time a fitter and turner was earning 59/1d, a bricklayer 65/5d. A GP £1,094 per annum and a clerical worker £192. The average working wage was 56/6d per week for males and 27/2d for females. A dozen terry nappies cost 7/11d, 100 Aspirin 1/6d, a pint of beer had gone up to 7d, a big bottle of lemonade 6½d, a pound of streaky bacon cost 11½d, a half pound bar of Cadbury's chocolate went up from 1/1d in 1933 to 2/- in 1935. A ton of coal was £1/3/11½d, a reproduction walnut bedroom suite cost a massive £40/19s.

It was about this time that Winifred's father died. A contemporary press cutting revealed that he lived at 2 Widey Villas, Saltash Road East, Crownhill, Devon:

> Mr Robert Ryder Stevenson, retired farmer, left £5,759, net £1,433. Probate has been granted to his son Ronald Frank Stevenson, farmer of Warleigh Barton, Tamerton Foliot and John Heywood of Lincoln Avenue, Plymouth. Mr Stevenson left a house to his daughter Ethel Daw, a house to his daughter Gladys Cottier for life, with remainder to her children, and a house to his daughter Ada Tincler with remainder to her son, Geoffrey and the residue between all his children.

None of the other children were mentioned by name and we can only assume that Winifred's legacy had been settled many years earlier. Barbara's cousin Geoffrey Tincler became an RAF pilot and was killed in the 2nd World War. His sister Yvonne became Barbara's best friend and later on her bridesmaid although she never herself married.

11. HOME FROM HOME

Glen Cot drawn in 1944 by one of the thousands of Services visitors

The outbreak of the Second World War was a difficult time for John as, being a fierce patriot coming from fighting stock, he must have been aching to go and "get stuck in". His immediate family did their bit, however. John's only two remaining brothers that were eligible for active service were Corporal Sandy Poole and Sergeant Walter Poole, who both served with the RASC.

Image 56

Donald had studied at Skerry College and subsequently joined the King's Company of the Grenadier Guards while Barbara enlisted with the WRNS as soon as she was old enough.

Image 57   Image 58

As someone who had to be always doing something, John had somehow managed to keep himself ticking over for a number of years, but stepped up a gear when he, as he put it, "found many boys wandering around" near their home and he and Winifred discovered the local RAF station had no NAAFI

canteen and there was no YMCA in the area either. Collaton Cross was home to the Devon Barrage Balloon Centre and a training centre for about 600 men of the Royal Auxiliary Air Force. There were thousands of personnel, both on active service and convalescing, at the local service posts, newly established gun sites and searchlight batteries all along the coast. As John wrote rather understatedly later, 'we took them in for an evening'.

Image 59

Their home in Riverside Road West was certainly a lovely place to 'rest awhile'. It was cosy and gleaming, full of his Army memorabilia, lots of clocks and an extensive collection of brass and copperware. Close to the naval ports of Devonport and Plymouth[49] it was three or four miles from Collaton to Newton Ferrers, down the formidable Newton hill. Once down the hill there was a t-junction with sharp bend to the left, along Riverside Road East past the Dolphin Inn and along to Bridgend. Turning right at the t-junction there would be another sharp bend, down another incline along to 'the Brook' which led to Riverside Road West. Because of the steep hill, bends and increasing narrowness cars would come down Newton hill and easily cause a bottleneck while they tried to manoeuvre their way back up the hill.

Image 60

---

[49] Devonport

88

John had, by now, acquired the nickname of 'Pop' and some even referred to him as 'the Professor'! The 'family' grew and its members were no longer airmen. They included sailors and soldiers from Poland, France, Holland, Norway, Australia, India, China and Malta and some only spoke a smattering of English. People would find their way to their cottage by hook or by crook, by foot, motorcycle, they would hitch lifts on service transport or go part way by bus. They came in small numbers at first, but once word spread of the hospitality they were given, the tiny cottage was never free of visitors. It is difficult to imagine how crowded it must have been. John was to write later[50],

> We had mattresses covering the entire floor of one big bedroom. Sometimes we had 18 or 20 sleeping there the night. From early morning until early hours of the next morning we made cups of tea and baked loads of cakes. We charged a penny for a cuppa and a penny for a jam tart, but a bed was free. We never shut the door to anyone right through the war.

The men and women didn't like eating and drinking at Glen Cottage[51] for free, so a small charge was made, which increased the number of guests even more.

John, being a methodical man, asked visitors to put their names in a book and to put in any comments they liked. Tributes, many of them ending in 'God bless you', soon filled the pages, along with sketches, drawings, poems and cartoons. The tiny cottage was alive with happy people when Nancy, Lady Astor, paid a visit in 1940. She wrote in the first visitor's book, 'thank you for this Home from Home'. Mickey Rooney visited in 1944.

The next chapter, Voices from the Past, is entirely devoted to the messages left by these brave people, many of whom would never return and a selection have been reproduced throughout the chapter. For the ones that survived, they would write after the war expressing their thanks and a wish to return, which many did.

So it was that in their modest way, John and Winifred were thus able to make a significant contribution to the war effort, albeit at arm's length, and

---

[50] In the Bristol Evening post, 23 July 1968 'Man Alive'
[51] Usually abbreviated to Glen Cot

threw themselves wholeheartedly into the task in hand, as he was to reflect many years later:

> *Once war broke out Glen Cottage became a refuge where off-duty men and women could find a meal and an easy chair to relax. We little thought that when war broke out and Collaton was enlarged that we would eventually have 20 years of airmen, soldiers and sailors of all nationalities, black, white and yellow, visiting our home.*

> In a Service canteen at Newton Ferrers Mr & Mrs Poole started a short time ago they have a box in which every grumbler has to put a penny fine. So far, various war charities have benefited to the amount of £7.

In fact the moaner's box mentioned above became a bit of a cause-célèbre in the local press. It wasn't just moaners; anyone who swore had to contribute too!

The Red Cross was sent the majority of the proceeds, but some money was siphoned off to send cigarettes, other 'goodies' and newspapers to groups of service-people on the front. Although, following his nasty experience, for the rest of his life John had a horror of cigarettes and his condition had finally been attributed to something other than smoking, he knew that "those poor devils out there" needed things like cigarettes to help them keep going. In fact, from the correspondence it is clear his son Donald was a smoker.

A visiting journalist from the South Devon Times wrote this moving article:

> Fellow Feeling

> This is a hard world and one suffers many disillusionments as one travels life's road. Occasionally, however, one sees a glimpse of something rare – the milk of human kindness which restores our faith in human nature and makes the world appear a better place to live in. Walking homewards along a riverside road last week, I came across a lady and gentleman who were busily feeding a stray cat with fish and milk.

> From a picturesque cottage nearby came the sounds of music and song. Several hours earlier I had passed that way and heard similar noises. Now the clock across the road pointed to eleven pm and strains of the National Anthem drifted through

the closed doors. "A club?" I enquired of my new acquaintances, "No", they said, "it's just a port of call for Service men".

I was then told the story of the Colour Sergeant, the man who, though still suffering from a throat wound – the effects of the first world war – found pleasure in, not only throwing open his doors to the RAF boys stationed nearby, but who also provided them with tea and sandwiches, making a home from home for many youngsters and keeping them from visiting the public houses which are the only alternatives, and for which they had no liking.

I heard of the man who cold be found outside the cottage in the early hours of the morning, thirstily gulping the morning air into his shattered lungs, and I wondered where he stayed while the fun went on. Did the atmosphere of a crowded room debar him from enjoying the company? "If ever a man deserved a medal, it is he", said my friend, and with that I thoroughly agree.

Only a few receive the medals, but hundreds of unknown others have also earned the right to wear one.

Image 61

Winifred was very much the driving force with many letters and acknowledgements being addressed to her. While John, in true Quarter-Master Sergeant style, controlled the budget and procured the provisions, neither of which can have been easy in war-torn England when every basic foodstuff was rationed to subsistence level. So John provided and Winifred was mistress of the kitchen, becoming celebrated for the quality of her baking. Teflon had just been invented and its marvellous non-stick properties would have made her life easier, as would the introduction of that wonderful keep-fresh invention Tupperware, but it is doubtful whether their pennies would have stretched to purchase such luxuries.

Neither would Winifred have offered the recently introduced chocolate chip cookie biscuit or the cheeseburger to her 'boys'; she certainly would not have had one of the new General Electric refrigerators with freezer compartment, content to make do with a meat safe with mesh door in the back yard. A food mixer would have transformed her life, but it was to be a few more years before the Kenwood food mixer would appear in the shops, or that necessity of modern kitchens, the microwave oven[52]. However, new-to-the-shelves Spam and Nescafé may well have been welcome additions to the Glen Cot store cupboard. Not everyone would have been partial to 'Pop's' old stand-by, Camp Coffee, with its flavour of chicory and strange smell which he loyally drank to the end of his days.

The Americans were finally drawn into the war when Japan attacked Pearl Harbour and this brought an influx of all sorts of US service personnel flooding into Glen Cot. What did they make of Camp Coffee? They certainly brought with them welcome and varied rations to add to the Pooles' pool of goodies.

Another, well-thumbed press cutting from the South Devon Times contemporary with the latter part of the war gave an excellent insight into the goings-on at Glen Cot. Again, no apologies for reproducing in full:

> A fisherman's cottage has been turned into a 'home from home' for men of the Services. Men stationed round about were poorly provided for, until Mr Poole and his wife got busy. Now, their guests consider themselves particularly fortunate for no canteen could give them the true home atmosphere they find here. Just before the war started Mr and Mrs Poole started to cater for visitors and now have several books filled with names of people who have been there, of all nationalities from all over the world. Then came the war.

> Troops stationed nearby started to drift down to their house, just a few at a time. So they started to make more and more pasties and pastries for them. They opened their home to the soldiers who come at all hours of the day and night. They can have whatever they want to eat and if they wish to, they can stay the night. Mrs

---

[52] Which, amazingly, was invented as early as 1945!

Poole does all the baking, but recently, when she was ill, the lads set to and baked all the pastry and there were no tragic consequences!

When we called at Glen Cot we found two lance-bombardiers and two privates, one of whom was saying goodbye because he had been posted away. He was laughing and chatting away in perfect English but he was Russian, said Pop. Soon afterwards, two bluejackets came in.

Asked if they wanted pasties or apple tarts, back came the answer straightaway: tarts! Over 600 tarts are made every week and they are a universal favourite. They are quite big and sell for a penny - just enough to pay for the materials used. Last year, bearing in mind the great demand for apple tarts, Pop laid the greater part of his orchard crop in store and so he is still able to supply fruit for the delicious tarts.

One of the sailors came from Canada and the other from Cheshire. There is a good piano, which is used quite a lot. "Often", said Mrs Poole, "we get a party of Welshmen here. Then we have a regular sing-song and their singing is wonderful". The rooms in their houses are low-roofed, small and very cosy and from the windows you look out onto the peaceful river scene. You can see fishermen mending their nets and Bill the boatman plying his trade. Mrs Poole is very fond of brass ornaments and the mantelpieces in both rooms are crammed with them. They are very brightly polished, too, for the 'boys' clean them regularly for her.

Mrs Poole showed us many hundreds of letters from service men, their wives and mothers, expressing their tremendous gratitude and appreciation for the work they have done.

On 20th June 1941 there was a thank you letter 'for the interest you are taking in the men from this camp' from the RN Commanding Officer at local Heybrook Bay. Finances obviously became tougher for them and on 24th November the Lt Col of the Army Southern Command in Salisbury wrote to say he was sorry to hear that they were thinking of closing the voluntary canteen, but could understand if they were bearing all the costs themselves. It probably did not help that Winifred was forever sending expensive packets of goodies to her 'boys' wherever they happened to be posted. The Lt-Col suggested that obtaining a catering licence would help them in their 'present predicament' and added:

> ... you have been kind and generous in your treatment of the men in your area and I take this opportunity of thanking you for your past efforts which must have

added very considerably to the comfort and happiness of the troops. Notification has been sent to the Ministry of Food.

On 29th November a letter came to Winifred, 'dearest Mammy' from a Polish lad, one of many, she had befriended. She was his 'best English mother' and he loved her with 'all of his hearth'[53]! He thanked her for the 'nice packet that Eddie brought with him from Glencot home'. It was signed 'your truly adopted son Jackie'. Among the hundreds of letters they must have treasured there was one from a Royal Australian Air Force Wing Commander stationed at nearby Mount Batten, thanking her for the 'excellent work' she and Mr Poole were doing. He was pleased to note that his 'chaps' were behaving themselves 'so well' at Newton Ferrers.

ھﮯھﮯھﮯ

RD/JP.

MINISTRY OF PENSIONS
NORCROSS, BLACKPOOL, LANCS.

Reply should be addressed to
The Secretary, Ministry of
Pensions, and the following
Number quoted.

Telephone : Thornton 2371
Telegraphic Address : --
Werpension, Blackpool

Ref No. 11/M/420686   17 August, 1943.

Sir,

In reply to your letter of the 5th August, 1943, I am directed by the Minister of Pensions to inform you that the Royal Warrant governing your award contains no provision for an increase at the age of 55 years or any other age.

Any grant by the Ministry in this connection is made under special sanction and is subject to the limitation that no addition may be granted which would increase the pension beyond the amount awardable under the post-Great War scale.

In your case comparison shows that your current award already exceeds the corresponding rate under the post-Great War scale, inclusive of the appropriate additions on

account of age and you are, therefore, ineligible for any higher rate.

I am, Sir,
Your obedient Servant,

for Secretary.

/account

Mr. J.J. Poole,
   Glen Cottage,
      Newton Ferrers,
         Plymouth,
            Devon.

Image 62

---

[53] Sic; presumably 'heart'!

On 17th August 1943 when he was 55, John received an answer to his letter to the Ministry of Pensions informing him that:

> The Royal Warrant contains no provisions for an increase at the age of 55 years or any other age. Any grant by the Ministry is made under special sanction. In your case, your current award already exceeds the corresponding rate under the post-Great War scale and you are, therefore ineligible for any higher rate.

Then why did the Pensions office write all those years back in October 1926 informing him that his pension would rise by 5d at the age of 55, and again by 4d when he was 65?

12. VOICES FROM THE PAST

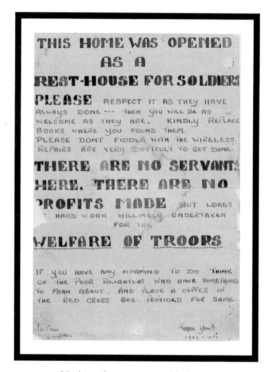

Notice, please respect this home

...the following are selected photos, messages,
poems and signatures from the visitors' books ...

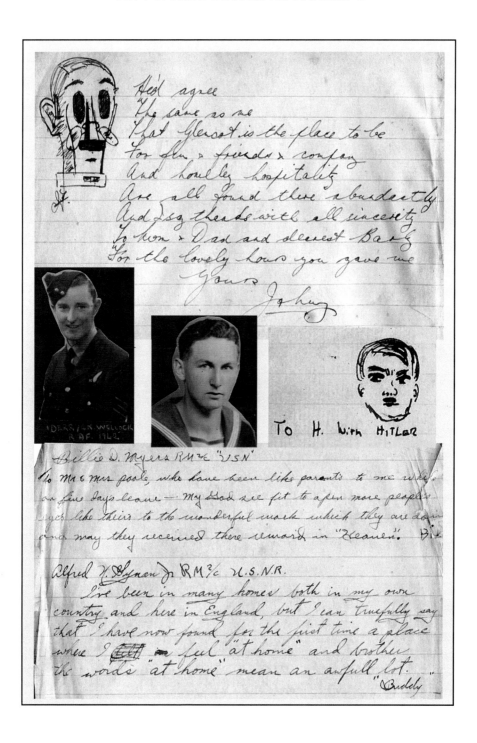

He'd agree
"The same as me
That Glencot is the place to be
For fun & friends & company
And homely hospitality
Are all found there abundantly
And I say thanks with all sincerity
To Mum & Dad and dearest Babs
For the lovely hours you gave me
Yours
John

To H. with Hitler

Billie D. Myers RM2/c "USN"

To Mr & Mrs Poole, who have been like parents to me while on five days leave — My God see fit to open more peoples eyes like theirs to the wonderful work which they are doing and may they received there reward in "Heaven". Bi

Alfred V. Synan Jr RM3/c U.S.N.R.

I've been in many homes both in my own country and here in England, but I can truefully say that I have now found for the first time a place where I feel "at home" and brother the words "at home" mean an awfull lot...
"Buddy

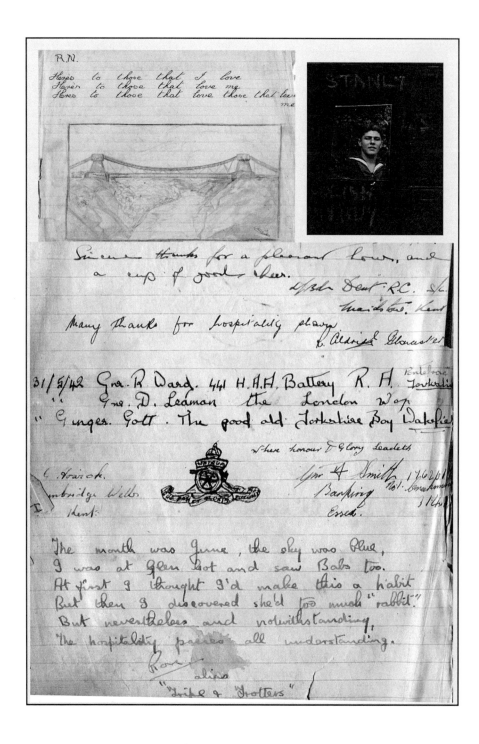

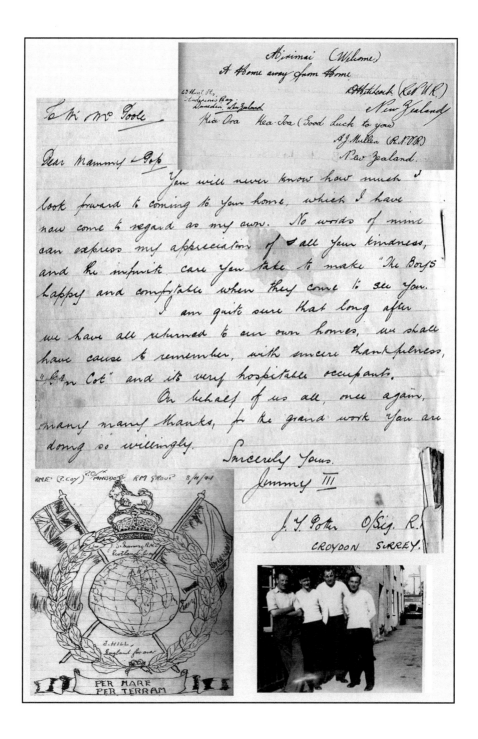

Airimai (Welcome)
A Home away from Home

Dittleback (Col U.K.)
New Zealand

40 Hunt St.,
St. Andyson's Bay,
Dunedin, New Zealand

Kia Ora   Kea Toa (Good Luck to you)

A.J. Mullen (R.N.V.R.)
New Zealand.

To Mr & Mrs Poole

Dear Mammy & Pop

You will never know how much I look forward to coming to your home, which I have now come to regard as my own. No words of mine can express my appreciation of all your kindness, and the infinite care you take to make "The Boys" happy and comfortable when they come to see you.

I am quite sure that long after we have all returned to our own homes, we shall have cause to remember, with sincere thankfulness, "Kia Col" and its very hospitable occupants.

On behalf of us all, once again, many many thanks, for the grand work you are doing so willingly.

Sincerely Yours.

Jimmy III

J.T. Potter   O/Sig. R.
CROYDON SURREY.

R.M.E. (P. Coy) P.O. (LANSDOWNE) RM GROUP 8/9/41

J. HILL,
England for ever

PER MARE
PER TERRAM

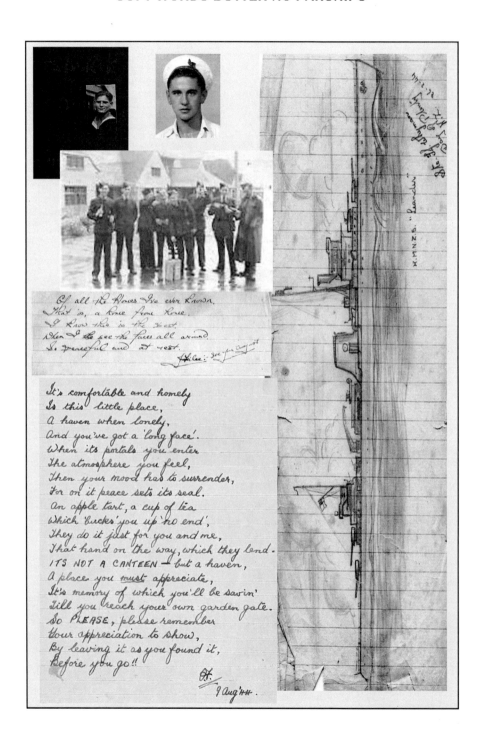

Of all the flowers I've ever known,
That is, a rose from Rose.
I know this is the best.
When I the see the faces all around
So peaceful and at rest.
Files: give for purpose

It's comfortable and homely
Is this little place,
A haven when lonely,
And you've got a 'long face'.
When its portals you enter
The atmosphere you feel,
Then your mood has to surrender,
For on it peace sets its seal.
An apple tart, a cup of tea
Which 'bucks' you up 'no end',
They do it just for you and me,
That hand on the way, which they lend.
ITS NOT A CANTEEN — but a haven,
A place you must appreciate,
It's memory of which you'll be savin'
Till you reach your own garden gate.
So PLEASE, please remember
Your appreciation to show,
By leaving it as you found it,
Before you go !!
H.
9 Aug'44.

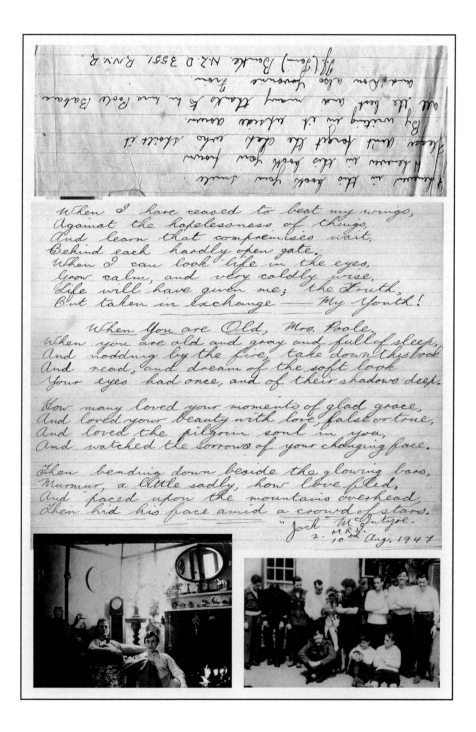

When I have ceased to beat my wings,
Against the hopelessness of things,
And learn that compromises wait,
Behind each hardly open gate.
When I can look life in the eyes,
Grow calm, and very coldly wise,
Life will have given me; the Truth,
But taken in exchange — My Youth!

When You are Old, Mrs. Poole.
When you are old and gray and full of sleep,
And nodding by the fire, take down this book
And read, and dream of the soft look
Your eyes had once, and of their shadows deep.

How many loved your moments of glad grace,
And loved your beauty with love, false or true,
And loved the pilgrim soul in you,
And watched the sorrows of your changing face.

Then bending down beside the glowing bars,
Murmur, a little sadly, how love fled,
And paced upon the mountains overhead,
Then hid his face amid a crowd of stars.

"Jack" McIntyre.
2. M.R.S.
10th Aug. 1947

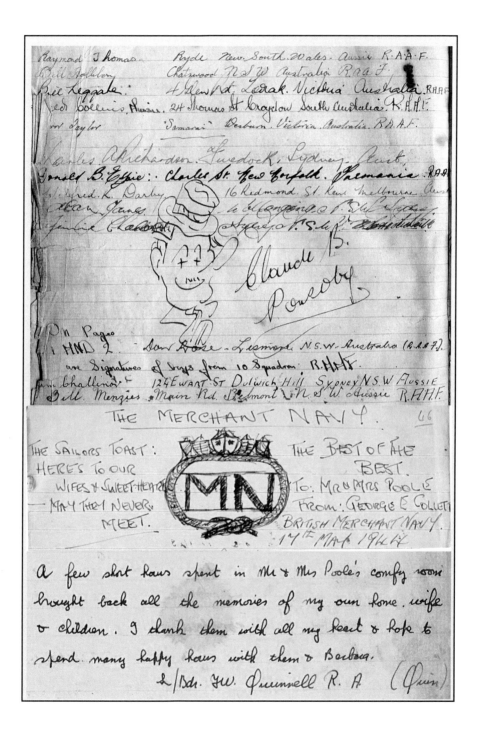

Raymond Thomas.   Ryde New South Wales. Aussie R.A.A.F.

Bill Rollston   Chatswood N S W Australia R.A.A.F.

Bill Leggate: 4 Glen Rd. Lorak. Victoria Australia R.A.A.F

Ted Collins, Aussie. 24 Thomas St Croydon South Australia. R.A.A.F.

on Taylor   'Samara' Desburn Victoria Australia. R.A.A.F.

Charles A Richardson. Swedock, Sydney. Aust.

Donald B. Gypie : Charles St. New Norfolk. Tasmania R.A.A

Wilfred R. Darby   16 Redmond St. Kent Melbourne Aus

Alan Janes   to Clangoire P Bel Sydney

Jimmie Clannerity   Sydney P S U Aust.

Claude B.
Ponsonby

On Pages

HND 2.   Sam Rose - Lismore N.S.W. Australia (R.A.A.F).

are Signatures of boys from 10 Squadron. R.A.A.F.

Jim Challinor   124 Ewart St Dulwich Hill Sydney N.S.W. Aussie

Bill Menzies Main Rd. Bedmont N.S.W. Aussie R.A.A.F.

THE MERCHANT NAVY.   46

THE SAILORS TOAST :   THE BEST OF THE
HERE'S TO OUR   BEST.
WIFES & SWEET-HEARTS   TO. MR & MRS POOLE
— MAY THEY NEVER.   FROM : GEORGE E COLLETT
MEET.   BRITISH MERCHANT NAVY.
    17th MAY 1946 47

A few short hours spent in Mr & Mrs Poole's comfy room
brought back all the memories of my own home. wife
& children. I thank them with all my heart & hope to
spend many happy hours with them & Barbara.
    L/Bdr. J.W. Quinnell R. A (Quin)

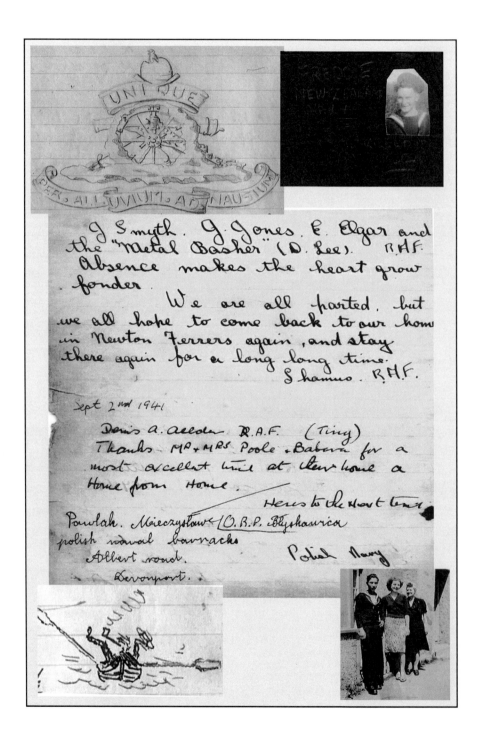

J Smyth. G. Jones. E. Elgar and the "Metal Basher" (D. Lee). R.A.F. Absence makes the heart grow fonder.

We are all parted, but we all hope to come back to our home in Newton Ferrers again, and stay there again for a long long time.
Shamus. R.A.F.

Sept 2nd 1941

Denis A. Allen R.A.F. (Tiny) Thanks MR + MRS Poole. Babara for a most excellent time at their home a Home from Home.

Heres to the Next time.

Pawlak. Mieczystaw (O.B.P. Blyshawica polish naval barracks Albert road. Devonport.

Polish Navy

No. 6293377. Pte. Tom Oram
7th Battalion (The Buffs).

FREDDIE & STAN

It is natural to us, for which the saints be praised, to soften the iron-shod foot of fate, by the hand of hospitality. Inarticulate to a degree, we best express our sympathy by five wondrous words, "Come and have a Drink."

Royal Balloon Barrage
861936. R.J. Gardner. August. 1941. Stanmore
Ro R.A.F.

John H. Connell
A.I.F. 6 Bt.

ora labor et ora
MCGS

Home is Best the place of rest
I love the Best
the places I have been North and South
But give me home for Ever More
God Bless them
7th Bn The Buffs. Both.
Mrs and Mr Poole.

Every time I go the home of 'mum + Dad' it makes me really cheerful, because it reminds of my own home + sweet, and I really must thank Mr + Mrs Poole for this pleasure, So I wish them All the Jolly Best. Harry Maffia.

105

You live for those who love you
Whose hearts are kind and true
For the heaven that smiles above you
And awaits your spirit too.
For all human ties that bind you
For the task your God assigned you
For the bright hopes left behind you
And the good, that you can do.

Ted O'Brien R.A.
Inverell N.S.W. Austr
Lynn Fitzgibbon 13A, R.A.A.O. Mount Ga
Ernest Mansfield Vic. Aus. R.A.A
James Wilson 7 Victoria Ave. East H
Snowy H.M.S FRENE

My sincere thanks to Mum, Pop & Babs for
they have done for me. Altho' my stay was
not very long, I shall never forget Glen
and the happy evenings we had together
hope that this is only "au revoir" and
we shall all meet again under more hap
circumstances. Until then, the very best
everything to you all. If you are ever
around my way the address is
14, Leslie Road
Toll Bar St Helens
Lancs,
and I only hope that I can make you
feel as much at home as you made
me.

Thomas Pender
R.E.M.E. 18

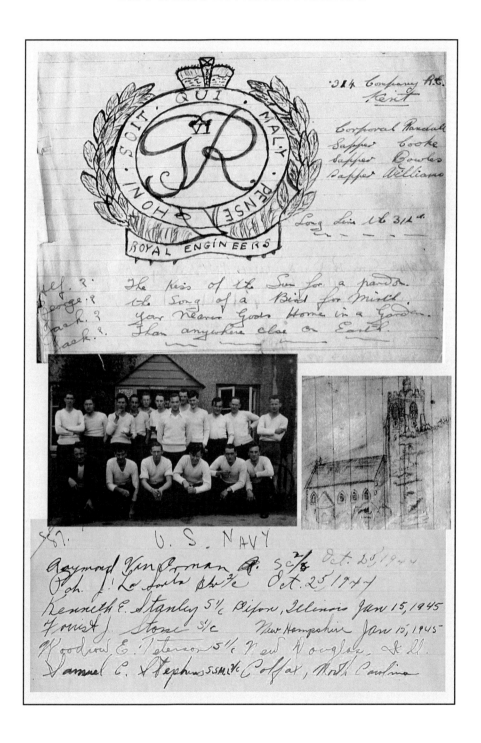

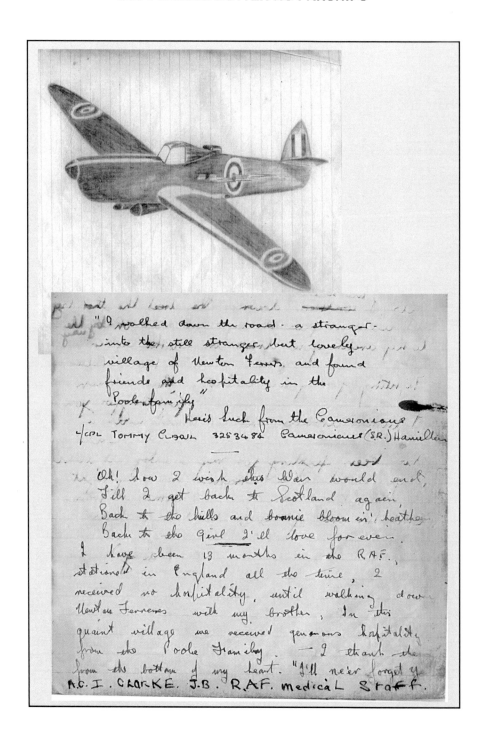

"I walked down the road - a stranger -
into the still stranger, but lovely
village of Newton Ferrers. and found
friends and hospitality in the
Poole family"

Here's luck from the Cameronians
L/CPL TOMMY CLARK 3253484 Cameronians (S.R.) Hamilton

Oh! how I wish this War would end,
Till I get back to Scotland again.
Back to the hills and bonnie bloomin' heather
Back to the girl I'll love for ever.
I have been 13 months in the R.A.F.,
stationed in England all the time, I
received no hospitality, until walking down
Newton Ferrers with my brother, In this
quaint village we received generous hospitality
from the Poole Family. — I thank them
from the bottom of my heart. "I'll ne'er forget you"
A.C.I. CLARKE. J.B. R.A.F. medical staff.

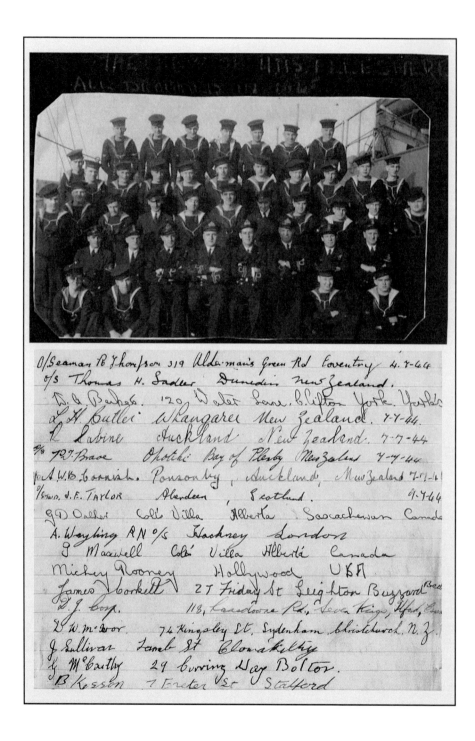

O/Seaman R Thompson 319 Alderman's Green Rd Coventry 4.7.44
O/s Thomas H. Sadler Dunedin New Zealand.
D.C. Barber 120, Water Lane. Clifton York. Yorks
L.H. Butler Whangarei New Zealand. 7-7-44.
R Labine Auckland New Zealand 7-7-44
O/s R.J. Brace Opotiki Bay of Plenty New Zealand 7-7-44
O/s A.W.B Cornish. Ponsonby, Auckland, New Zealand 7-7-44
O/Stwd J.F. Taylor Aberdeen, Scotland. 9-7-44
G.D Oakley Coll Villa Alberta Saskachewan Canada
A. Wayling RN O/s Hackney London
J Maxwell Coll Villa Alberta Canada
Mickey Rooney Hollywood USA
James Corkett 27 Friday St Leighton Buzzard Beds
L.J. Coop. 118, Lansdowne Rd, Seven Kings, Ilford, Essex
D.W. McIvOr. 74 Kingsley St, Sydenham Christchurch N.Z.
J Sullivan Lamb St Clonakilty
L. McCarthy 29 Curving Way Bolton
B Kisson 7 Freter St Stafford

Heres to folk with Golden hearts.
All The Best & lots of Luck
Yours / A.R.Kennedy.
Captain

When you are gone and there is left nothing of
Of what we were, or what we did and said:
And all of you will meet and leave unsought
The souveniers we loved the books we read:
No tears we ask nor sighing recollection spent
Upon the heedless world—but only this:
That we who talked and laughed with you
talent upon the precious hour, the cheek to kiss
Regretted not one moment of our stay
Nor laid our heads to rest in sorrows arms

R.N.F.

Thank you for the happiness
Although we soon may part
I'll have the memory of Shen-Col
To carry in my heart
My loved ones left me years ago
& none can take their place
But meeting Ma & Pop & Babs helped
fill that empty place
Happiness we cannot buy
The best things have no price
So thank you dear for giving me
a glimpse of Paradise

R.H. Arnold

This is the best time I had since I have joined the army.

Gnr H S Shale.
525 Battery S/L R.A.

W/O	R.H. Duckett.	London S.W.11.	11.5.46.
F/O	R.Phipps.	Harrow Middlesex.	11.5.46
S/Ltn(a)	Z.B Hurell	Haversfield Glos.	11.5.46.
3/o	Geoffrey M.R. White	Anstell, Lytham-St.annes Lancs.	11.5.46.
F/o	B. Gilman.	Wildman Rd. Plymouth.	11.5.46.
W/O	Davies. T.	Edinburgh. Scotland	11.5.46.
F/S	M' neale	Watford	'' ''
W/O	W.Williams (Ace)	Bury St Edmunds.	'' ''
W/O	M.D. Camdon.	Fort William & Glasgow.	8.7.46.
W/O.	Robert S Bamberger.	Barkingside, Essex	8.7.46.

To MUM

THANK YOU & GOD BLESS YOU FOR PUTTING ME ON THE ROAD

THAT HAS BROUGHT ME THROUGH.

NEARLY 7YRS AGO TODAY WE FIRST MET BUT ETERNAL

TIME CAN NEVER ERASE THE GOLDEN MEMORIES I HOLD.

SOME-DAY I HOPE YOU WILL VISIT MY FAMILY, SO FOR NOW IT

IS AU REVOIR, NOT GOODBYE,

LOVE JOHNNY.

13, ORCHARD PLACE,

FAVERSHAM, KENT.

You must have a wonderful heart, for the kindness you have shown to the boys, God Bless you. how I would have love to have met you. we were so near and yet so far. never mind, there will come a time some day. I cannot express my feelings enough for the kindness you have given to my son L/Cpl. A. H. Morse. 6294233 The Buffs. and I know other mothers must feel the same about you.

From a greatful

Mother.

They will always be an England while their are folks like these

R.N.

A friend in need. Is a friend in ded" Many thanks for hospitality & grand cup o' tea! Frank Fawcett.

Roger Lang.

I saw a lovely poster
"Join the R.A.F. and fly",
So I joined last September
'Twas a case of "do & die"
Now I'm in the Service,
With a suit of Airforce blue,
It's simply amazing
The binding jobs I do!

The list of trades is varied
To read 'em all you'd tire,
Ground gunners on a post
With guns they never fire
Police who are lawless
Bashers who don't bash
Cooks who cook all kinds of food
Which always ends as hash!

Our crew are the lads
Who Per Ardua ad astra
Spare a thought
Now & then
For a poor Cook house dishwasher!

Thanks a million
all the same
Mr & Mrs Poole

W. J. Levett (Jack)

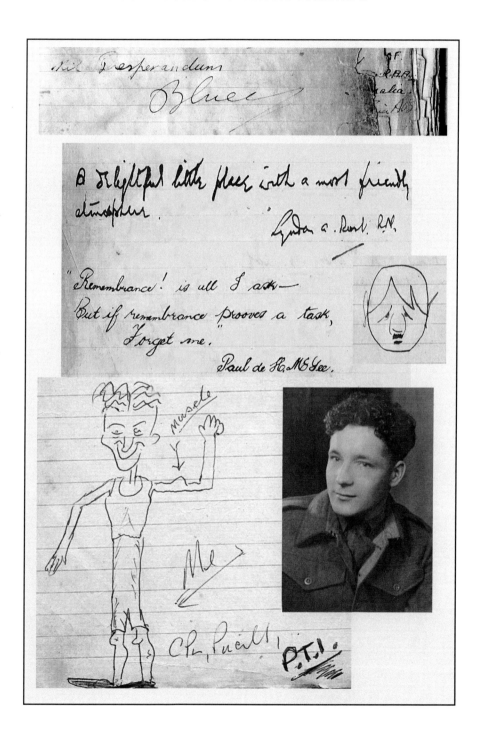

SOFT WORDS BUTTER NO PARSNIPS

If there's room for me in this book
There's room for me in your heart
There's room for both of us in heaven
Where true friends never part. *Stokers D Kay, RR Evans, J Wright, L Williams*

I walked in solemn silence in a dull dark cloak – awaiting the sensation of a short, sharp shock – from a cheap and chippy chopper – on a big black block – But then I found Mrs Poole. Many, many thanks. *Wilf Darby, 10 Squadron RAAF, Melbourne, Australia*

The Airman's Lament

The poor airman lay down a'dying
As under the wreckage he lay.
The mechanics they gathered to listen
As his last dying words did he say.
Take the piston rods out of my back-bone
The connecting rod out of my brain.
From the base of my spine take the crankshaft
And assemble my engine again.
G. Ladbrooke, 929984 LAC Mount Batten, Plymouth, 20 Dec 1942

We left 'Aussie' on Anzac Day (1942) bound for the Blighty shore.
And here we are in the land of beauty. *Cpl D Cook, Narrabean, NSW, Australia, Cpl F L Masters, Worgan Hills, Western Australia, 10 Squadron.*

When the golden sun is setting, and your thoughts from cares are free
And of others you are thinking, will you sometimes think of me?
Gnr J Cairns, Bonnie Scotland

When climbing the hill of prosperity may you never meet any old friend falling down.
God bless you and your loved ones. *AC W/1 Walker E, Collaton Cross, WAAF*

England for ever. Wales for one day longer. *Vivienne Stacey, WREN, Cwmrhydyceirw*

When months and years have passed you by and on this page you cast your eye
Remember it was a friend sincere who put these lines of remembrance here.
George Punnouris, RAAF, 66 Bays Water Road, Kings Cotts, Sydney NSW

Have destroyer, have a yacht. But station me at old Glen Cot. *Walter Watkins, LDG/S70 HMS Onslow*

During two years of Army life and all the incumbent hardships caused thru' not only Army short-sightedness but civilian stupidity I have found an oasis of sanity – Glen Cot. *J C Bowdery*

Up the Marines and Navy. *J K Henderson, RM, J Tidswell RM*

What! Write in this book? Where? Ladies look and gentlemen spy.
Not I, I'm shy. Goodbye (but I'll be back again).
Stanley H Howe, RAAF, Adelaide, South Australia

Lonely years we've spent apart will soon be ended now.
The face I've seen through lonely tears will soon be near my heart.
When I come home again, the warmth of your smile will dry all our tears away.
When I come home again, the years will not seem as long as they do today.
Though we have waited so long for the day, parted no more dear, I come home to stay.
When I come home again, Memories will take the place of our dreams today.
E Lewsley 29th May 1949

Royal Marine Eng: The work is hard, the pay is small, so we do our best and bless them all. *Marine Wakefield, George Kenneth, Berkley, Marine J Large, High Wycombe, Bucks, Marine Scott Russell, Halifax, Yorks. Marine S M Williams, Warrington, Lancs*

To Newton Ferrers, the Pooles and all I've known here, *au revoir* (but not goodbye, I hope). I shall never forget the good times I have had here. All that I would like to say in appreciation I find impossible to put down in words. Ever yours, *Sorrowing Paddy*

You ask me to write in your album, I hardly know how to begin,
but I wish you joy in simple things, in friendship, books and flowers
That every day, in every way be filled with many happy hours.
Thank you Mr & Mrs Poole, for the most wonderful time I have had since I have been at Collaton. *Vernon S Wickland (RAF) 46 Ashbournham Rd, Greenwich, SE10. March 4th, 1943.*

Who stole the pasties?

You live for those who love you, whose hearts are kind and true
For the heaven that smiles above you, and awaits your spirit too.
For all human ties that bind you, for the task your god assigned you.
For the bright hopes left behind you and the good that you can do.
Ted O'Brien, Inverell, NSW Australia

To Mr & Mrs Poole, who have been like parents to me while on a few days leave. May God see fit to pin more peoples' eyes to the wonderful work which they are doing and may they receive their reward in heaven. *Billie D Myers RM 2/c USN*

Food like the Ritz, far from the Blitz, four miles from 441 HAA Bty RA.
Gnrs Butterworth JHR, C Ford, R Beasby, Jimmy Perkins

We take the opportunity of thanking Mr & Mrs Poole for the kindness and generosity they have shown us. The apple tart and cooking is the best I have known, and I always tell my friends to visit Mrs Poole when they want relaxation and comfort, not forgetting the peace and the neighbourhood. In Glen Cot, one finds warmth and happiness, when life gets you down. I am truly thankful, my friends told me of this lovely abode. Thanks again Mrs Poole, while people like you exist, England will never fall to the enemy, that includes Barbara and Mr Poole too. Thanks a million. *Ord. Seaman F Yates, RNVR and Ord Seaman D Fradgeley, RNVR*

This house is like my own home although it is far away I shall always think of my wife no matter what happens. Please God get this war over. Thank you for a quiet seat and a good read. *George Stubberfield, London*

13. LOST IN FRANCE

Donald Iliffe Poole on parade

On 13th May 1943 John and Winifred's son Donald sent a postcard with 'good luck' on the back, postmarked Malton, Yorkshire. A little inappropriate, he wrote, but it was the best he could get in the village shop. It bore an optimistic printed message, 'good luck never comes amiss, so cheerio, I'm sending this. May it bring you luck in every way, and lots of it for every day!' On the back was overprinted the cheerful words of the Prime Minister, 'Let us all strive without failing in faith or in duty'. He also sent a postcard depicting the West Front of York Minster, 'Here for the weekend, not too bad. All the best, write soon, Love, Don'.

The first letter on file from Donald was postmarked Gilling East, North Yorkshire but he headed it 'somewhere in England, 1pm'. He had been on 'a Scheme' and it had been a strenuous week, during which time everyone in the Platoon had got mail except him. He was very disappointed but knew his parents must have been 'very busy'. He gave an indication of the type of menu they faced each day but that they did all the cooking themselves, so it wasn't 'too bad'. They 'mashed down'[54] at least six times a day.

They had no contact with the outside world and, although it could be exciting at times, for the most part there was a lot of 'hanging around'. Time to make a bit of mischief:

> Our lot caught a duck yesterday and the Commanding Officer came around on inspection this morning and just as he was passing the scout car it started to quack. What a do! He told our despatch rider to take it back to the farm where we got it from. So we tied a label around its neck saying 'returned with thanks after one night in action'.

That they were about to move into active service was revealed by a few little sentences. In the first one he half-jokingly advised his parents not to write any secrets to him because the mail was going to be censored in future. The second said simply, 'this is a very big exercise indeed and we are just a small part of it'.

A subsequent letter apologised as Donald had now received from them one parcel, two letters, one with a postal order, and two other letters. Winifred had obviously sent one of her celebrated food parcels as he wrote: 'the lard,

---

[54] Made tea

butter tea and sugar made all the difference between a good and bad start. The blokes were pleased with it and I'm authorised to say from my crew of 8, thanks a lot'.

Image 63

A few more postcards followed with light-hearted greetings along the general theme of 'keep smiling and don't worry'. Then a gloomy letter came from him. No 3 Company, I[st] (Motor) BN, Grenadier Guards, Mere, Wiltshire. Dated Saturday. Donald had 'lost his stripes' and it seemed like the end of the world. He had returned 50 minutes late from leave and was placed under close arrest.

> Oh, my remorse is something awful. I don't know what you must think of me but I know I'm thoroughly ashamed of myself. If all goes well and I work hard I hope I will get them back again before I come home on leave. I'll try hard for all your sakes and another thing Mum, I hereby solemnly swear to you that I'll never touch another drink. Please don't think too badly of me please as I'm absolutely fed-up.
>
> Could you come up for the day Mum please next Saturday or Sunday and I'll meet you at Frome. I so badly need you Mum. Please come and bring Babs if she can come. This may seem childish to you Mum but what's the use of a mother if you can't tell her your troubles. That's all of mine for the present and I hope the last. Don't tell anyone Mum for a bit, as I'll try hard to get them back. Your loving son Don (Gdsm).

Losing his stripes and being demoted from Corporal to Guardsman would continue to devastate him throughout the rest of his life.

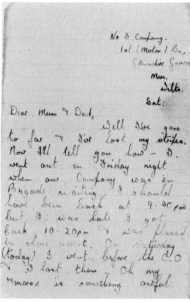

Image 64

Donald's next letter to his mother was plaintive and very raw. It was dated 'Thursday', from Warminster, Wiltshire. Winifred was a strict teetotal as it was against her religion[55] and it seems that her reaction to his 'bombshell' had been accusatory, he had been guilty of drinking heavily. Something not unusual amongst young recruits in the Army (and young people everywhere, come to that). He was trying to reassure her and buck up her spirits:

> Dearest Mother, I hardly know how to begin this, but I suppose I must. Your accusations are nearly all true Mum, but you mustn't take the blame for me.

They were obviously very close. She was missing him and had serious misgivings about his enlistment. He reflected on his young life with a mixture of sadness and regret.

> God alone knows what has happened to me since I've been in the Army. The reason I expect is that I had such a sheltered life until I was 16. Then suddenly I was chucked into this world and that's the reason. Obviously at 16-19 one is very impressionable and I got my impressions away from home, in this Army with the wrong blokes. I don't remember much from 16-17; I wasn't quite on my feet.

> Nowadays I'm quite OK and all your fears are quite unfounded about me. I've never been drunk in my life and never want to be either. If you think all these things Mum, and I agree there are some foundations. Your suspicions became facts and you keep brooding on them. Please don't think I blame you, because I am your only son. You wanted me to get on, which is only natural, but I haven't, not through any fault of yours Mum, but mine, all mine. You've been the best Mother any boy or girl could wish for.

---

[55] Plymouth Brethren

SOFT WORDS BUTTER NO PARSNIPS

He was debating whether or not he could face coming home on leave as he felt he would not be able to look anyone in the face. He would get a 'nagging from Dad' and would have to 'bluff people'. He sensed that maybe Winifred didn't want him to come home this time either, probably for similar reasons. He added sadly, 'I've grown away from you, haven't I, but still each day I think of you and home'. He added, rather prophetically,

> I wonder whether I shall altogether escape this ghastly war and get back to pick up the threads. Or shall one of us be dead and all that is left be bitterness and regret and a mound of earth or a name on a War Memorial. How I hate myself for writing to you in such a way but if it explains even a little of my past I shall be more than happy.

Winifred's letter must have really struck that invisible chord within him, because Donald ended his letter trying to reassure her further:

> Mum never, ever, think or write such things again. You are not an old woman, 42 is not a great age. I know you have been through hell but if anything happened to you, Mum, I would never, ever forgive myself, so please regard me as your desire to go on living. I'm not very great or very good but for my sake and Babs' too. Please try. I haven't been a good son to you Mum, not in the sense of the word. But now it's your time. Ask and you shall receive anything that is in my power to give you. Think it over, Mum, please and don't ever worry about me again. Your devoted Son, Don

Heart-rending stuff, but there was more to come.

Don wrote again from Mere (this time No 9 PL No 3 Company) to 'Mum, Dad and Babs' that at last he had some news which he had 'worked hard' to bring about. For the last two months he had set about 'working to the standard of manhood of an NCO in a battalion, who may have to depend on its very existence on its NCO's'. He had taken his punishment 'without a squeak' and hoped and prayed that the day will not be long distant when he could wear his chevrons again 'with honour'. He had worked on his career, on Schemes, on parade and off and his shooting had improved[56]. In fact, when they were firing 5 rounds at 200 yards distance with respirators on, he scored 5 bulls, 'real, pukka bulls dead in the centre'.

---

[56] Donald won a bronze medal for rifle shooting

'In short', he wrote, 'I have done everything I could possibly do to elevate myself'. He had achieved two official credits and 'quite a few' unofficial ones and his commanding officer promised that he would be made up at the first opportunity, although at that particular time they had too many Corporals.

> I had peace time ideals not war time, all these have been given the push and it's a lot better. I have bags of real friends. You can easily tell them, the rats always desert the ship. All mine stood by when I was going down, but now I'm on the surface again. I'm due on leave on Thursday, but shan't come. At least it seems hardly fair to you to have me home after I've let you down. If you write back and say it's OK I shall only wear civvies all the time. I don't want pity, justice only.

He added poignantly:

> I hope and pray the day will not be long distant when I can wear my chevrons again with honour. There is time for me yet, remember I am just 20.

The next letter was again from Mere in Wiltshire and written in early August 1943. They were coming to the end of their training and Donald took the opportunity to send Winifred a card and letter for her birthday:

Image 65

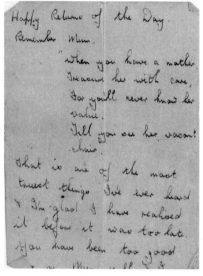

Image 66

When you have a mother,
Treasure her with care,
For you'll never know her value,
Till you see her vacant chair.

This is one of the truest things I've ever heard and I'm glad that I have realised it before it was too late. You have been too good to me Mum really and I hope and pray that I shall be able to reward you in the near future.

I know I can never repay anything that you have done for me, but when this war is over and I come home out of the Army I'll make amends. Nothing I have done yet has been any good I know, but I have my life before me. If God spares me I shall make my life something worthwhile after all.

At present I'm so bitter against the Army for whom I've given 4 years of my life - wholeheartedly without reserve. That one man had it in his power to take away the little that I was so proud of. What did he know of my hopes and ambitions, small and insignificant as they may have seemed? To be a Sergeant at 20 was one of my chief desires. Even to be a Corporal at 20 is now denied me. If only he knew what unhappiness those three words 'revert to Guardsman' caused one man I think he would be rather surprised even shocked slightly if he is at all human.

He ended the letter in his characteristic way, 'Don't worry about me, I'm quite OK'.

Image 67

All went quiet until an impersonal 'field services post card' arrived at Glen Cot, dated 28th June 1944. He was obviously across the Channel and had entered the Theatre of War.

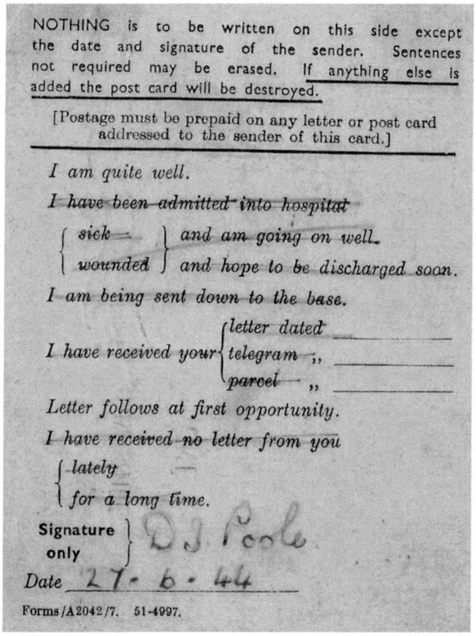

NOTHING is to be written on this side except the date and signature of the sender. Sentences not required may be erased. If anything else is added the post card will be destroyed.

[Postage must be prepaid on any letter or post card addressed to the sender of this card.]

I am quite well.

I have been admitted into hospital

{ sick } and am going on well.
{ wounded } and hope to be discharged soon.

I am being sent down to the base.

I have received your { letter dated _____
telegram ,, _____
parcel ,, _____

Letter follows at first opportunity.

I have received no letter from you
{ lately
{ for a long time.

Signature only D J Poole

Date 27 - 6 - 44

Forms/A2042/7. 51-4997.

Image 68

The next communication was dated 10th August, 1944 - Passed by Censor no 11443:

Dear Mum and Pop,

Haven't received the cigs yet but they are usually delayed. Still, I've plenty at present and am not grumbling. The weather is still ideal for our kind of war and we see bags of air activity around. The country is very hilly and hard fighting ground as you may guess, but we get by. I find it increasingly hard to write letters without mentioning the war. I don't want to write about it but it's our chief topic of conversation.

Did you get plenty of rumours in World War 1 Pop? If you're anything like us you did. Really fantastic rumours are accepted at their face value. Our platoon's funniest one was that we were going to New York to show the Yanks what a British lot looks like. The really funny thing is that at least one person believes it. If there is a chance of moving, bets are placed forward or back. We took a small town some time ago and had just finished clearing it when we were shelled. I had to laugh because one of our chaps said, "it's OK, it's our shells". It appeared we'd moved too fast & cleared it sooner than expected. There were no casualties so we could afford to laugh.

At the same time we had a funny 'do'. We were in our slit trenches just watching when we saw about 40 planes overhead. Everybody was quite pleased, then all of a sudden we saw the black crosses. Needless to say it's the first and last time I've seen such a great deal of the Luftwaffe. They only stopped about 5 minutes and then flew away at a frantic speed when they saw our spotter coming. That's probably all the planes they have and were trying to impress us. The persons one feels most sorry for is the French civilians who are very good to us. Everywhere we go (especially now when the Bosche is showing his true colours) we are treated very well.

I hope this letter helps to show you what has been happening to me in past month or so. I can't tell you more for obvious reasons but I'll remember all the best bits and tell you. God bless and don't worry. Don.

SUPREME HEADQUARTERS
ALLIED EXPEDITIONARY FORCE

Soldiers, Sailors and Airmen of the Allied Expeditionary Force!

You are about to embark upon the Great Crusade, toward which we have striven these many months. The eyes of the world are upon you. The hopes and prayers of liberty-loving people everywhere march with you. In company with our brave Allies and brothers-in-arms on other Fronts, you will bring about the destruction of the German war machine, the elimination of Nazi tyranny over the oppressed peoples of Europe, and security for ourselves in a free world.

Your task will not be an easy one. Your enemy is well trained, well equipped and battle-hardened. He will fight savagely.

But this is the year 1944! Much has happened since the Nazi triumphs of 1940-41. The United Nations have inflicted upon the Germans great defeats, in open battle, man-to-man. Our air offensive has seriously reduced their strength in the air and their capacity to wage war on the ground. Our Home Fronts have given us an overwhelming superiority in weapons and munitions of war, and placed at our disposal great reserves of trained fighting men. The tide has turned! The free men of the world are marching together to Victory!

I have full confidence in your courage, devotion to duty and skill in battle. We will accept nothing less than full Victory!

Good Luck! And let us all beseech the blessing of Almighty God upon this great and noble undertaking.

Dwight D Eisenhower

Image 69

126

SOFT WORDS BUTTER NO PARSNIPS

Donald was obviously a regular correspondent, and so was his family. On August 20th, 1944 he wrote to Barbara thanking her for her last epistle. He said that Winifred managed to write to him every day although he knew how busy she was. He had obviously just heard about his cousin Geoff:

> So Geoff is presumed killed in action. What a rotten thing war is. If they knew where his plane crashed I might be able to locate his grave at least. Was it over Germany or France? I suppose it's all very vague. Will soon be in Paris. God bless and keep writing. Your devoted brother, Don.

On 27th August he wrote a happy letter home explaining that the NAAFI car had come again which 'breaks the monotony'. He was able to buy 'chocs, biscuits, cigs, razor blades and hundreds of other small needs of a soldier'. The buoyant mood turned to reflection as he wrote:

> The only time I feel really homesick is when I see scenery like ours. Sometimes some of it is so much so I imagine I am home. When one is fighting there's no time for sentiment. It's just kill him or he'll get you.

> Still holding the Yealm Regatta? Who won the crabbing boat race? I shall always remember those races and the feud between the villages. These are the things one remembers long after war is a memory. Memories of dances and hiding behind curtains! Of breaking your old teapot, your operation, bathing at Allan's, picnics all the summer, biking in the autumn, dancing in winter, kids' parties, Barbara's burnt anatomy on a lamp whilst getting ready for a party. Millions of things come flying through my mind and help such a great deal. Don't worry Mum. With parents and a sister like mine, I'm sure to be back. God bless you all, your devoted son, Don.

On the same day he wrote to Barbara.

> Went to a French cinema today - it seems as though that's all I've been doing, but believe you me I've had a busy time. Our air force is doing a magnificent job Babs and don't let anyone tell you they're not. They have bags of guts and according to prisoners they fear the RAF a terrific amount and so they should. Most of our boys have a strong feeling of contempt for the lauded Luftwaffe which only comes out at night - just as well as our Spits would certainly bring them down. Must get this off to the censor now, kid, as it's nearly time. Don't worry, I'm OK. God bless and good luck Babs. Tons of love, your brother Don.

The last letter on file was dated 28th August, exactly a week before he was wounded. He teased Barbara about the red, white and blue envelopes she had been putting her letters in, 'where on earth did you dig them up?!' He wrote about a friend called Johnnie, an Irish Guard who had just been wounded and sent back to England. The censor had, rather obviously, scrubbed out the actual figures in the next sentence:

> Our Platoon has been very fortunate as regards casualties up to present, XX killed and about XX wounded. I had a letter from Pop today included in a pack of papers. Also a comb so I'm pretty lucky now as regards the hair situation. You may keep the toasting fork until I come home and then - boy oh boy!

> It's time to eat now so I must finish. I honestly think a soldier would be lost without his mashing down kit - tea making apparatus to you! God bless Babs, your loving brother, Don.

Call it sixth sense, or whatever, but Winifred knew something was up and had already begun to experience daily premonitions in the shape of a white cross at the bottom of the front garden. Official notification then came that Guardsman Poole had been posted as missing, then came the letter to say he had been wounded by a 'gunshot wound to the right arm and body'.

Finally on 29th September she wrote to the Commanding Officer of the 1st Motor Battalion to try and put an end to her torment. Her worst fears were confirmed when a handwritten letter arrived from Captain Heele, the Adjutant, dated 3rd October, who had

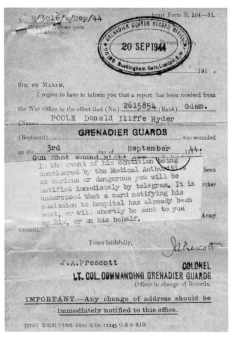

Image 70

himself just received notification that her beloved son had died on 5th September:

> Guardsman Poole has died of his wounds he received on 3rd September and has been buried in an American Cemetery in France. He was originally wounded during the advance into Belgium when he was taking part in a very gallant and successful action against one of the few places in which the Bosche held out against us on the day we got to Brussels.

He had been in the army for just six years.

It had taken exactly a month to hear the confirmation and much longer to be told officially, in fact so long that Winifred took up the issue with the authorities in the hope it would help to minimise the agonies suffered by others regarding the fate of their loved ones.

Having seen the type of letters Donald had written with his delicate combination of candid soul-bearing and jaunty optimism, such finality must have been devastating for John but even more so for Winifred. Someone called 'Beaky' was quick to react with a postcard dated 9th October and the words 'all my loving thoughts are with you'.

Image 71

A letter from Major Baker, dated 26th October explained that he was given the news of Donald's death when one of his men returned from an American hospital. He wrote:

This battle was the culminating point of the GAD's advance into Brussels. We ran into the enemy and attacked. Your son was killed during the attack, which was a complete success and enabled the Division to reach Brussels that night. Your son had been in my Company for a long time. I liked him immensely and he was a great asset to us. He was a first-class wireless operator and in battle he always set the boys around him the very highest standard of courage and bravery. He was absolutely fearless.

My very deepest to you in your very tragic bereavement.

On 1st November Henry Studholme wrote to Winifred to say he had spoken to the Adjutant about her 'boy' and put the whole matter 'in his hands' and 'you can be certain he will find out everything there is to find out'. On 2nd November the official notification came via copy of a letter to Mr Studholme – exactly two months after Donald was killed. The copy letter from Asst Regimental Adjutant, Grenadier Guards said immediately after they had received Mr Studholme's letter of 1st November they received a wire from 2nd Echelon saying Gdsm Poole had died of wounds on the 5th September in an American Medical Unit and had been buried in an American Cemetery at Champigny[57] in France. He added:

Image 72

It would have been better had the Adjutant not replied to Mrs Poole's letter, but he had no reason to suppose that the 2nd Echelon would take 2 months to report that Gdsm Poole had died of wounds.

A press cutting around this time mentioned that John and Winifred had been officially notified that Gdsm Poole had been wounded in Brussels subsequently died from his injuries. It went on to say:

---

[57] In fact, it was the village cemetery at Villeneuve St Georges, 18km from Paris

... much sympathy with Mr & Mrs Poole and their daughter Barbara (serving with the WRNS) has been expressed in the village. Mr and Mrs Poole run a popular canteen for the Services in Newton Ferrers and they have received letters of thanks and appreciation for their work from all over the world.

Winifred realised that had she not taken the initiative and written she may have had to wait even longer for the official word. The Adjutant had doubtless put himself in her position and replied to her unofficially as soon as he knew something, as any caring human being would have done. Straightaway she wrote to Henry Studholme who wrote back on 3rd November 1944, 'your boy must have been a splendid fellow'. He wanted to take up this issue with the War Office and explained to her that it was not the regiment that were at fault here, it had been the 2nd Echelon. Difficulties in communication were compounded by the fact that Donald had been wounded at a time of 'very rapid advance' and had been taken over by an American medical unit.

On the 10th November an official letter arrived:

CERTIFIED that according to a telegraphic communication received in this Department that No 2615854 Guardsman Donald Iliffe Ryder Poole, Grenadier Guards died of wounds on the fifth day of September 1944 while serving with the Allied Expeditionary Force in North West Europe. Dated this Tenth day of November 1944. (Signed) A Mercier, the War Office.

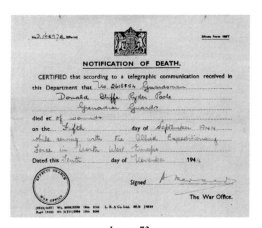

Image 73

On the 15th November another letter arrived from the diligent Mr Studholme, postmarked The House of Commons. He had discussed the matter about the delay in notifying relations about casualties with the Parliamentary Private Secretary to the Secretary of State for War. He explained:

> ... there were unfortunately a few cases like yours during the time of the advance into Belgium and Holland, the reason being that the movements of the armies were so rapid. Men were left behind in hospitals, which also sometimes moved, as of course did also the man's unit. So in some cases it was very difficult for the hospitals to make contact through the official channels through which the official notification must come to the relatives.

He reassured her that by her writing she had no doubt 'helped to emphasise the point' and added that he was so very sorry that they should have had 'all this agonising uncertainty'.

Brigadier E H Goulburn DSO, Commander of the 8th British Infantry Brigade, BLA wrote personally on 16th November 1944:

> I am very sorry indeed that your son, Guardsman Poole, was killed in action with the 1st Grenadiers. I have up till recently been commanding that Battalion and I know you will understand why I have not written before when I tell you how busy I have been.
>
> Your son's death is a loss, not only to my own Battalion, but also to the Regiment. He had proved himself to be a most excellent soldier, and set a fine example of calmness and courage in danger, to those around him.
>
> We here realise what we owe to him, and the others, who have fallen in action. I have had such loyal and splendid service from my Battalion, both at home in England and out here in action, that I feel that the least I can do is to write and tell you this.
>
> It may be some consolation to you to know that we appreciate your son's fine qualities and what we owe to him for what he has done for the Battalion. May I, once again, offer you and your family my deepest sympathy in your sad bereavement.

A hand delivered letter was received from Buckingham Palace:

BUCKINGHAM PALACE

The Queen and I offer you our heartfelt sympathy in your great sorrow.

We pray that your country's gratitude for a life so nobly given in its service may bring you some measure of consolation.

George R.I.

Image 74

Soft words butter no parsnips, indeed.

ৠৠৠ

Still, as John would have said, "life has to go on". In January 1945 the Ministry of Pensions increased his pension to 16/11d pw for life backdated from 5/1/44 to 30/1/45. This must have been small comfort but would have allowed them to give more to others. And early in 1945 there was a letter from the commanding officer of Donald's platoon, the King's Company, 1st Battn Grenadier Guards thanking Winifred for two more parcels of papers etc that were very welcome during the 'long rail journey through Germany'. Another quite chatty letter followed (marked 'on active service') thanking her for the parcel of periodicals.

In May 1945 Germany surrendered and America dropped atom bombs on Hiroshima which led to Japan's surrender.

John was presented with the Defence Medal to add to his Long Service and Good Conduct Medal.

This war, too, had taken a terrible toll. It is estimated that 35 million people were killed in the Second World War, Russia again coming off worst with 18 million. In the wake of the war the United Nations was founded, as was the IMF, the International Monetary Fund.

In July 1945 Capt Lock of 1st Btn Grenadiers wrote again apologising for not writing earlier but hoped Winifred would understand the difficulties. He added, 'there are not many of us left now who were there when your son was', but that the younger ones were 'building up to the standard very well'. A further letter thanked her for the various gifts, especially cigarettes, also ping-pong bats and darts - a typically generous and caring thing to do and he sounded genuinely touched, 'they are certainly the most needed items of indoor games out here'.

On 19th February 1946 a letter was received from the Officer Commanding Grenadier Guards in reply to Winifred's of the same date. He could 'appreciate very well' what her feelings must have been and was sorry that they could not have been more help to her. 'Only today' he wrote, 'certain of your son's personal belongings[58] have arrived' and promised to forward them. Sadly none of the things that she had mentioned previously to him were among them.

Image 75

On 27th February 1946 Barbara had received word from 'George' that he had located her brother's tomb at the village cemetery at Villeneuve St Georges. Donald's corpse had been brought there by the British Services and was 'probably found in the Senart forest or in the surroundings of Mélun'. George managed to find a lady who would 'take them around'. So it was that in September 1946 Winifred and Barbara made what was for both of them a pilgrimage via Ostend to Paris to visit grave number 94.

---

[58] New Testament bible, pictures and photographs, letter, designations (3) coin, identity disc, newspaper cover

The conundrum remained. How could a soldier who was taking part in the final advance into Belgium who was wounded, apparently tended by an American mobile unit, who died a few days later and whose body was subsequently retrieved from the Senart forest, came to be finally interred in a private cemetery 18km South West of Paris? John and Winifred must have been a bit confused at the official version as it just didn't seem quite logical, but what is logical about war anyway?

On 21st December 1948 Henri François who lived in Paris XI made the trip to visit Donald's grave. He wrote, 'we have laid flowers there in remembrance of all the nice things you have done for us' and he took a photograph. This photograph shows the grave with proper headstone as it was when Barbara visited again in May 1988.

Image 76

135

14. BOUQUETS AND BEGINNINGS

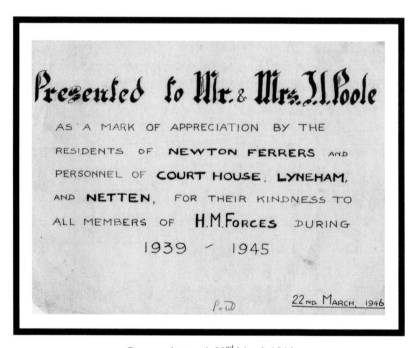

Presentation card, 22nd March 1946

The end of the second World War did not mean the end of the Pooles' activities at Glencot, far from it. However, on 22nd March 1946, a presentation was made to them by Ian Spooner, the Commodore of the River Yealm Yacht Club, on behalf of the residents of Newton Ferrers. John was given a cheque and Winifred a gold watch. In fact, the 'canteen' was still going strong because the demand was still there from the service personnel still stationed around and about but many had been demobbed. One of the Polish Navy chaps, Eddy Gronowski wrote to Winifred from Paris, 'here I am dear Mummy writing you this few lines to let you know that I am well demobbed and leaving[59] in France'. Barbara had spent her late teens/early twenties surrounded by thousands of men but she finally found the man of her dreams when she met Flight Lieutenant Albert Howley 'Witt' Wittridge.

He had been at RAF Collaton Cross recovering from a broken back resulting from a 150mph 'prang' just after the war when he had been patrolling the oil

Image 77

---

[59] Sic, living

lines in Israel. He had just happened to come across Glen Cot and as it was quaintly put at the time in a press cutting: 'he came for a cuppa and won himself a wife'. It had been love at first sight.

Image 78   Image 79

The winter of 1946-1947 was one of the snowiest and most severe on record, but on 22nd January in the breathtakingly beautiful setting of the Church of the Holy Cross Barbara and Witt got married.

The groom's mother, Beatrice (far left in the group photo), had travelled from Teddington in Middlesex to see her dashing Spitfire pilot son get married, and there was an RAF guard of honour. Winifred is next to her in the photo, and John second from the right. Also in the picture are Barbara's cousins Yvonne, Gwen and Edna.

> The bride's father is well known locally because of the canteen which he ran during the war and for the kindness and hospitality he displayed to the many thousands of forces who passed through his hands.

ۋۋۋ

A lady called Jill who had served with the ATS in 480 unit had been a frequent visitor to Glen Cot and had married an RAF pilot who was shot down and imprisoned in Germany. After being demobbed they returned to her home county of Surrey but she continued to write many letters to John who could always be counted upon to be a good correspondent. One letter thanked him for the custard powder, raisins and golden syrup. She ticked him off for toiling all the way up the steep hill to the post office in order to post it to her. She enquired about the petrol situation, and was John still able to go out fishing? Three years on, it was evidently still a time of rationing.

On 25th March 1947 Winifred received a letter from the Company Commander of the Army Cadets in Barnstaple, 7th North Devon Battalion. He had been commander of the cadets since the inception of the cadet movement in north Devon and her remarks, he said, had been 'very encouraging'. They had obviously been a well mannered crowd of boys when they visited Glen Cot!   In April John's pension stood at £4/10/8d per week, having just been increased by 5s.

May of that year might just have marked a high point in John's life. A hand-delivered letter arrived at their little cottage.

I was informed recently that during the last War you and Mrs Poole opened up your house for the use of all members of His Majesty's Forces during their 'off time and leave' and provided meals for them at a very small cost, and that over 60,000 availed themselves of your magnificent hospitality. I write, therefore, to tell you that I have brought the above facts to the notice of His Majesty the King, who hears of your generous hospitality with great appreciation. I must also send you my heartfelt sympathy in the loss of your only son in the Grenadier Guards.   Yours truly, (signed) Fortescue.

Image 80

Earl Fortescue was the Lord Lieutenant of Devon and John had several copies of this important letter made (photocopying wasn't done then – it involved finding someone with a typewriter and making a good copy as errors couldn't easily be corrected). On a few copies John had scrawled:

1959 – 70,000 people. We closed our home in 1959 when the RAF Rehabilitation Centre closed. All done with love over 20 years.

SOFT WORDS BUTTER NO PARSNIPS

৯৯৯

Virginia Stephanie Anne Wittridge was born in Barnstaple on Remembrance Day, 11th November 1947. Lynda Annys followed a year and four months later, on 23rd March 1949, born in the little upstairs bedroom at Glen Cot. We can only imagine that both events gave the grandparents great joy.

Although the first disposable nappies had been introduced to a waiting public, it is doubtful whether something so revolutionary would have been used in the Poole - Wittridge household! Across the other side of the world, the country of Israel had been established and its capital moved to Jerusalem. Also, the Dead Sea Scrolls were found, the Polaroid camera was invented, Chuck Yeager broke the sound barrier in the Bell X-1 rocket plane, and Mikhail Kalashnikov invented the fearsome AK-47.

৯৯৯

In 1953 John's pension was increased by an extra 4d a day subject to good character. He had begun regular correspondence with a number of newspapers. One of them, the Sporting Record, replied to one of his about the merits or otherwise of the Arsenal football team (he was a devoted Plymouth Argyle fan). In 1958 John's total pension seems to have shot up: 'war pension £4/5s' including unemployability supplement, comforts allowance, PI Warrant and SRA, wife's allowance, and age allowance and totalled £11/3/6d.

An important looking invitation arrived in the post. The Daily Mirror had instigated their own New Year Honours list, each person receiving a gold medal for their services to humanity. As the paper put it:

Image 81

It is for those people who, in the ordinary

way would have no reward at all. They are not famous people. They have no titles. Most of them have little money. But they are all people someone was proud to know. People you will be proud to know too. They have been named for their courage, their devotion or their unselfishness. They are men, women and children who have earned more than titles. More than a gold medal. They have earned the gratitude of their fellow-people.

Winifred could well have been reticent about going along and was always much happier for John to take the limelight but she must have known that without her huge energy and dedication none of this would have come about. She could well have been impressed by the panel of judges: Lady Pakenham, Canon L J Collins and Sir Tom O'Brien MP and the most influential and high profile of newspaper journalists and 'Agony Aunts' at that time, Marjorie Proops, she of the immaculate coiffure and trademark cigarette holder.

Image 82

Another Donald, 'Speed Ace' Donald Campbell was the fifth judge and he also made the presentation.

Image 83

He was to die some nine years later on 4th January 1967 on Coniston Water when Bluebird flipped 30ft in the air while he was attempting to beat his own world speed record of 267 mph.

141

Image 84

There was the usual handful of press cuttings to mark the special event.

Two Newton Ferrers Citizens Honoured – Mr & Mrs Poole had been selected from thousands nominated by Daily Mirror readers and on Wednesday 22 January Mr & Mrs Poole were presented with a Gold Medal, inscribed on one side 'in recognition of a Service to Humanity' and on the other side, 'The Daily Mirror Award 1958'. They were invited to a dinner at the Waldorf Hotel and stayed two nights. The citation was that they 'kept their doors open to Servicemen, providing meals for 70,000 at a nominal cost and they still have people in daily from the RAF Rehabilitation Centre, Collaton Cross'. In doing this work, Mr & Mrs Poole felt that not only was it a noble thing in itself but in doing this they are doing honour to the memory of their only son Donald killed in the latter days of the war.

15. DOWN BY THE RIVERSIDE

"One of the happiest times in my life"
JIP fishing off Newton Ferrers

Newton Ferrers in the late 1950s was not quite the tourist trap it is today and it had not yet been designated an Area of Outstanding Natural Beauty but it was slowly becoming a visited place. Following the second World War and with the motor car becoming within the reach of ordinary families, Newton Ferrers had to gradually gird its loins and make room for the seasonal influx of tourists. From as early as the 1930s as road accessibility improved, the locals began to feel the stirrings of disquiet regarding the ramifications of tourism to their quiet way of life.

John was the steward of the reading room, a splendid but rather gloomy space with an atmospheric smell. With this position came a tied cottage situated opposite which was adjacent to Glen Cot. As part of his daily 'duties' John read the barograph, making a careful note of the pressure and placing that information plus the tide tables on the notice board outside which was invaluable information for the local fishermen and sailors.

Image 85

Built in Victorian times the reading room was in its own garden leading down to the river Yealm. It had two opulent but fading billiard tables with overhead fringes and easy chairs for relaxing. Not that children were allowed in there, but there was a treasure trove of 1920s silk shoes, dresses that would set a young girl's heart racing, stuffed rather unceremoniously in stout boxes behind a velvet curtain to the right hand side of the stage, and the right era for them to have been Winifred's.

Until the facility at Collaton Cross finally closed down, Winifred made the long trek up Newton hill and along to the base where she worked part-time as a storekeeper. Fiercely independent, she bought herself a scooter and all went well until the fateful day she returned home, black and blue, the scooter scraped and mangled. She had dragged it all the way home having

come off it and fallen into a ditch. The scooter was never repaired but Winifred mended well.

Winifred was broad Devonshire, and called loved ones "me 'ansum" and female members of the family she called "maid" rather than "darling" or similar. She used to sit her grand-daughters down and solemnly impart to them all sorts of gems such as "a man peeks 'ees sweetheart by 'er 'ayd and 'er 'eels" and the more prosaic "if you've got relaxation, you'm

Image 86

got the greatest gift of all" to the more curious, "it's a man's playce to arsk and a lady's to refoos." As you can imagine, none of it meant much to 9 or 10 year old kids.

Living over the road from the river, a lot of John's daily life was bound up with the sea, in one way or another. He had an eighteen foot motor boat (the 'big' boat) with its inboard Kelvin diesel engine, and a wooden dinghy (the 'little one') that Virginia and Lynda delighted in rowing, once they were taught how, of course.

Just like Granddad and their mother Barbara, they loved the water too. It was a short distance away from the house and to access it, they would run

Image 87

across the little road, through the gate marked 'private', across the reading room garden, and then through to Glen Cot's own little oasis. On the right there was the small garden house, with kitchenette and bedroom, crammed full of furniture and homely mementoes. Turning left there would a hedge-lined path leading to the private quay.

Witt promised both daughters 2/6d the moment they completed the huge (for them) swim across the river, which was probably about a quarter of a mile - and back - which they eventually managed, and it was at Newton Ferrers that they both learned to ride bicycles.

Image 88

The quay was the scene of Lynda's first brush with death where, while crabbing at high tide, she fell into the river between the rowing boat and the high stone wall (above, right) and Virginia managed to pull her to safety.

In addition to the fantastic front garden, there was a back yard with a privy which, in the 1950s was still gainfully employed. It was well stocked with a pad of carefully torn-up newspaper impaled on a hook. The top of the planked wooden door was finished with a row of VVVVVs which gave one something to focus on instead of the cold and dark. Up some steep steps carved into the bank, following an ash-strewn path bordered by a low box hedge, there were some blackcurrant and gooseberry bushes, then the bountiful vegetable plot with the lines of produce standing to attention in neat rows. At the very back of the garden were the chickens, nondescript brown things that loved scrabbling around the apple trees for the corn and scraps John allocated them. Feeding the chickens was another thing like the winding of the clocks he carried out as though his life depended on it.

John and Winifred loved the tick-tock of clocks, the more the merrier. Both houses were full of them and a cacophony of ticks greeted the visitor. The way in which John lovingly wound them and regulated them was typical of the prescribed way he ran his life. So although there was a certain compulsion, rigidity and control about him, he was not stern and always had time to indulge his grandchildren, and any other children for that matter. He loved the noise and laughter of young people and had quite a playful nature. So playful, in fact, that Barbara recalled that when she was a teenager John had a tendency to conceal himself up trees and lie in wait for her and her friends whereupon he would jump down and half scare them to death!

Security was paramount to John, and food was security. As befits an ex-Quarter Master, he was an astute sourcer and buyer. His store cupboards were a sight to behold with row after row of canned fruit, cream crackers, sterilised cream, tea, Camp coffee (yuck), tinned pink salmon and crab, dried peas and beans. He would have had a wonderful time with the modern day BOGOF's[60]. There seemed to be an almost imperceptible delineation when it came to who cooked what. While Winifred would do the fancier things and the baking and John, wasting nothing, would prepare masses of stews and curried dishes on the terrifying but redoubtable coal range, an art or science in itself which he managed seamlessly and effortlessly. It never seemed to go out and was always hissing or smoking to show that it was alive and well, but as he was always up at some ungodly hour it was unlikely that anyone would have seen him light it in any case!

Image 89

He was always busy, busy, busy, but found time to escape in the big boat to line fish, either alone or with other fishermen, neighbours or one of the grandchildren. Bass, pollack and mackerel were standard and delicious fare, and there was always plenty to go round. On hindsight, he must have either been very brave or very foolhardy as, had he fallen overboard, it would have meant certain death once water entered the small hole in his neck.

---

[60] Buy one, get one free!

SOFT WORDS BUTTER NO PARSNIPS

Image 90

When he couldn't, didn't or daren't go out, there was more often than not a fish gift of some kind, or some vegetables placed on their front door step. It was his job to cook any fish or shellfish. Lynda remembers once looking on in horror as a part-boiled lobster lifted the lid and managed to escape from the huge, bubbling pan. It fell onto the hotplate, clattered to the floor and was just making its clacking getaway when, alerted by her screams, John rushed into the kitchen, scooped it up and put back. How could anyone eat lobster after that?

He used many little phrases - like "there's a difference between laughing and splitting your face" a sanitised version of "farting and splitting your arse" - many of which have been faithfully remembered and put on the right hand side of each page. Although he was a little prudish and had deeply held convictions of moral issues, right and wrong etc, he was nevertheless a basic, no-frills personality.

Polly the African grey parrot was a case in point who lived in a large cage by the kitchen window and loved to watch what was going on outside. She used to suffer from indigestion and enjoyed pecking at her daily Rennie. It was interesting to surmise how John managed to teach her to speak when he could not, but she somehow replicated many of his little phrases. "Kiss Polly's bum" was a favourite utterance! Unfortunately, she would also copy his impressive array of farts, doing it so well, so loudly and so often when people went past the window, that it was something that the whole family grew to anticipate and accept. People reacted in a host of different ways and the neighbours, particularly Aggie and Walter Baptie next door, made sure they weren't in close vicinity when tourists walked by lest they be blamed.

Image 91

As if by magic at the end of the day, Polly's activities would cease the moment her blanket was placed over the cage. But even parrots don't live forever and when she finally breathed her last he was, by all accounts inconsolable for days.

Image 92

In common with most seaside villages, the social culture had grow up around the sea, and 'Pop's' little empire became the epicentre of the most important function of the year, the annual Regatta, where his information and knowledge would become crucial to the safety and success of this event. Not

149

surprisingly, Barbara had grown up a water baby and was swimming and rowing champion for many years.

Things hotted up a bit towards the end of the 1950s. John took a trip down memory lane and made the long trek north to his old Regiment at Berwick-Upon-Tweed where he met many of his old comrades who, rather surprisingly, all thought he had been dead for the past 30 years!

ৡৡৡ

With the closure of the RAF Rehabilitation Centre there seemed little point in continuing. It was the end of an era. The end of the canteen that John and Winifred had kept going for 22 years, "seven days a week, 52 weeks a year, including Christmas Day". Their job was over and they were probably at a loss to fill that gap in their lives; what to do next? Barbara, Witt and children were a few hundred miles away and this could well have been a deciding factor. So it was they began to wind down most of their voluntary work.

Image 93

John subsequently gave notice that he was giving up his stewardship of the reading room (and with it the tied cottage), a position he had held for 36 years. Mr Derek Hockaday succeeded him as steward. He reluctantly gave up his fund-raising activities with the RNLI and received a letter of appreciation for 30 years' work. The Honorary Secretary of the River Yealm

Regatta expressed grateful thanks for their kindness during Regatta Week – every year for 30 years'.

There seemed to have been quite a knees-up at the Yealm Yacht Club in Newton Ferrers the night the village turned out in force to honour their well-loved citizens. A presentation was made of a flower basket, a warming pan and two haggis and the Yealm United Football Club gave them an oil painting of a local scene.

John was Newton Ferrers Swimming and Youth Club's first benefactor and a keen supporter and he made a final prize draw at the reading room amid a vote of thanks from all concerned. Vicar the Reverend Grimes paid tribute to them for their kindness in 'lending their home to the Services' and presented Winifred with gold watch.

The Welfare Committee of Newton Ferrers had pushed for John to have proper recognition and duly wrote to the Prime Minister. On June 24th 1959 the Prime Minister's Secretary confirmed that

Image 94

Mr J I Poole's name had come up for recommendation in the Birthday Honours List. 'The number of good candidates exceeded the number of limited awards available' he wrote, but promised that John's name would be amongst those 'which will be put forward for consideration in the New Year list'. But it didn't happen next year either and must have been a bit of a blow. Jill had written some years previously:

> I think I speak for all of us when I say you of all people should get something in the way of recognition for your kindness to the thousands of us who met you. Some have short memories but others do remember, and those are the ones who will never forget. I well remember running short of cash but there was always a cup of coffee and an apple pie and a free look at the papers and a retreat from some of the cruder types in the army who at times made life hell for us. I think you will get an OBE, but as you know it all takes time.

MR. J. I. POOLE

Farewell Presentations at Newton Ferrers

After 36 years as steward of the Reading Room at Newton Ferrers Mr. John Iliffe Poole of Glen Cot, Riverside Road, has retired.

He and his wife have gone to live with their married daughter at Bristol.

Before they left, presentations took place at a social evening at the Reading Room on Saturday evening. Mr. Gordon Foster, committee chairman, gave a warming pan and two haggis—half of the members, and Mr. Wilfred Bending, secretary, gave an oil painting of a local scene. From Yealm United Football Club, Mr. B. Ferrier presented an ornamental flower basket, and Mrs. Poole was given freesias.

Mr. Derek Hockaday is to be the new steward.

Image 95

Sadly, he was never to receive that sort of recognition, made all the sadder as he was to spend the rest of his life helping, advising and inspiring fellow laryngectomees.

16. CAUSE FOR CELEBRATION

The Lord Chamberlain is
commanded by Her Majesty to invite

Mr. J.Y. Poole

to an Afternoon Party in the Garden of Buckingham Palace
on Tuesday the 23rd July 1968, from 4 to 6 o'clock p.m.

Morning Dress or Uniform or Lounge Suit

Garden Party invitation, 23 July 1968

John and Winifred's plan to make the move to Bristol crystallised when they found out that Barbara was pregnant for the third time. To uproot and move was a bold decision for a couple of pensioners (John was then 71), especially when they had been so deeply entrenched in their life and charitable works in Newton Ferrers. Being local celebrities, there was a flurry of press cuttings.

Donald Albert Wittridge was born on 3rd December 1959.

Image 96

Up the road, the cottage John and Winifred had bought, 66 School Road, Frampton Cotterell, had to be gutted and modernised to their taste including state-of-the-art metal Crittall windows. They must have felt like fishes out of water leaving such a small, close-knit community for the relative anonymity of a rather unattractive sprawling north Bristol village. The fact that they were a few hundred yards from their daughter, her husband and by now three grandchildren must have kept them going in the hiatus between the newness of arriving with boxes and suitcases and a degree of emptiness, until they were at the very least on nodding terms with neighbours. But being warm personalities, they soon built up a good relationship with those around them.

They were generous to a fault, and plied special visitors like teenage granddaughters with food, either main meals of lamb chops with rich gravy, fish and chips, or a cup of tea and a piece of angel or Battenburg cake, Jacob's crackers and Edam cheese or toasted sandwiches (made with a circular sandwich maker on the hotplate of the Aga), field mushrooms on toast with a dark, well-seasoned sauce.

A wonderful example of John's irreverent sense of humour was to go into the butcher's, make sure a bit of a queue had built up behind him and then ask for a quarter of a pound of "old maids' memories"[61].

Tea bags were still a novelty at that time[62] and they fitted in nicely with John's cut-and-come-again philosophy - from time to time a few had been glimpsed hanging up to dry on the little clothes line in the back yard! He did explain such hoarding on many occasions with a one-liner that went something like, "well, I had a wife and two small kiddies to bring up on a pension of £2/18/9d". He never expanded on this stock phrase, and of course, no-one questioned him further, perhaps sensing that the answer would not be comfortable for him or the asker.

They lived two doors from the local primary school and John was always a magnet for children. He loved them, as did Winifred. It bugged him that at sports day there were no cups or prizes awarded to the children, so he made sure the winners had cash prizes and he presented a shield each to be used for subsequent boy and girl sports champions. Of course, it wouldn't be done today, but he used a portion of his pension every week to buy bags of every imaginable sweet, and then stand to attention at end of school time, to hand them out via the teachers who all patently adored him. It goes without saying that the children thought he was wonderful too and they called him 'Pop the Sweetie Man'. He kept of a sheaf of letters written by the children. One in particular stands out.

> Dear Mr Poole - I hope you're still rich after you sent us that money. We are very grateful. The class is very grateful for the sweets. It is playtime now so goodbye for now.

With his funny voice and noisy breathing and usually dressed in hat and raincoat, nobody thought there was anything untoward. Surprising, really.

John began to develop networks within the local medical fraternity and became a frequent visitor to the ENT departments of hospitals in Bristol and Gloucestershire, forming a bond with a cancer nurse from Frenchay Hospital, Mrs Phyllis Panes, who went on to get an MBE for her sterling work with

---

[61] Chipolata sausages
[62] Although they were actually invented in 1904

larygenctomee patients. Together with speech therapist Judith Foot they founded a Lost Chords club in Bristol, followed by a second. Lost Chords clubs were springing up in Birmingham, Leeds, Glasgow, Plymouth and overseas.

So it was from about the early 1960s onwards that John was to really capitalise on his experiences to inspire others. In those early days of pioneering but relatively crude medical treatment of having one's throat opened and voice box pulled out, it must have felt at worst like a death sentence, at the very least like your body had been mutilated and your masculinity/femininity compromised. Let's make no bones about it, the whistling, wheezing noise of air being sucked in through a half inch hole in the throat was noisy and most people would whir round to see who or what it was. Dr W Morrison may have been gilding the lily a little to imply that it was not a noisy process.

The late, great actor Jack Hawkins had a distinctive, gravelly voice but he, too, was similarly affected by throat cancer and had to have 'the op'. One cannot imagine how he felt when his trade-mark, his greatest asset, had been taken away and he worked hard to source the best possible synthetic voice box, but it was a relatively primitive affair and unfortunately made him sound a bit like a dalek (Dr Who was all the rage then). John didn't like the idea of "mucking around with things" and he used to shake his head and say, "no good will come of it". Mr Hawkins unfortunately did not survive long after his operation.

Neither John nor Winifred reacted well to having time on their hands and although they did not seem to have really found deep contentment within each other, they seemed to rub along without rocking their little boat too much. The odd flare-ups would come from John having made a comment in his inimitable way, being asked to repeat it again and again by hard-of-hearing Winifred, culminating with both getting red in the face and she with a wave of her hand turning away, mumbling resignedly, "I can't hear what you're saying...". This was a familiar pattern. He would then mutter that she was "deaf as a post". She used to have agonising headaches, they would be called migraines these days, for which she always carried repulsive (but presumably effective) smelling salts. She also swore by a daily dose of Andrew's Liver Salts (to keep her 'reg'lar').

Migraines are often as a result of stress and John, with all his punctuality and certain way of doing things, must have been quite exasperating to live with at times. However, it may have been that she was too much of a free spirit to have been restrained by his regulatory strictures. Where she wasn't so free was in the area of religion. She was teetotal and quite Victorian about anything relating to wine, women and song.

Although he was to get more and more involved in charity work, he still found time for his shopping expeditions. In his mid 70s he crackled with charged-up energy while she was only in her early 60s and in fading health. They were in the new house about a year when they celebrated their 40th wedding anniversary on 1st June 1961. The various headings in the press told the story, '40th Wedding Anniversary - Hospitality to the Services'. 'Op Man 40 Years Wed'. 'Couple Married for 40 Years', 'On Borrowed Time – 40 Years of Marriage'.

The reason for Winifred's lingering melancholia had to be the loss of Donald, although she never talked about him. A year after their 40th anniversary there was a letter from the Commonwealth War Graves Commission about copies of the 'relevant section' of the Commonwealth Roll of Honour at a cost price of 7/6d each. Entry 2615854 Donald Iliffe Ryder Poole.

The longer time wore on, the more interest grew in John's medical case as he was becoming a bit of a cause-célèbre in those circles. On 23rd October 1963 he received a letter from Mr Malcomson, Consultant ENT Surgeon at Frenchay Hospital:

> Mr Guthrie's wish is to have a photograph of the patient who holds the record, if not the world record, of an active and useful life (40 years) after the Laryngectomy, to be put in the Royal College of Surgeons in Edinburgh.

It was possible that the 'original diseased organ' was in the College of Surgeons Museum in Edinburgh, and this would be 'of considerable value' for the purposes of teaching surgeons. The end of another era came with the death of Sir Winston Churchill in January 1965, and the Christmas card from the KOSB proudly depicted this auspicious event; they were detailed to guard the coffin. In April 1965 John travelled to Eltham to attend a get-together and take part in the parade of the 29th Division Association, offering to pay for his 15/- lunch.

With any spare time that he might have had, he initiated a fourth career as a newspaper correspondent/charity worker, having been initially a soldier/quarter-master, then a patient/advocate, then a catering manager/favourite uncle. He had never been a stranger to publicity, having been a public relations consultant long before it became fashionable. It wasn't self-promotion as much as publicising 'the cause'. The cause in this case was justice for anyone oppressed and campaigning long and hard for better education and awareness of the whole painful business of throat (and any other cancer, for that matter). He thought the medical profession were skilled in keeping hard facts from people they thought couldn't take it and they were a little too "knife-happy" into the bargain.

If a little outspoken, John was a shining example of personal empowerment, a message he wanted to convey to anyone who would listen; "If I can do it, surely you can. Get off your arse and try". Anyway, from this time forward he began to correspond on an even more regular basis to papers and magazines the length and breadth of the country; any subject that he felt strongly about would do. Rita Marshall of the Daily Express wrote:

> What a lovely letter! My father had a Laryngectomy operation seventeen years ago. He thinks he is one of the 'oldies'. I don't think I dare tell him about you! Like you, my father visits patients who are about to have this operation. It's a splendid feeling, isn't it, when you can help somebody out and prove to them that life can be just as normal after the operation.

All good things must pass. In July 1966, perhaps prompted by Winifred's continued melancholy, they decamped back to Devon. This, of course, generated further press coverage, 'Frampton Cotterell says Farewell to One of its Best Known and Courageous Residents'. They bought a semi-detached house in Fort Austin Avenue on the 1930s estate on what had been her family's land. He called it 'Auld Reekie'[63] and after getting the house to their liking, John set to work to get the garden shipshape, including rows of vegetables just like his garden at Newton Ferrers, planted with military

---

[63] Nickname for Edinburgh old town because it often appeared to be covered by a cloud of reek or smoke

precision and establishing a colony of passion flowers to climb up the wall. He resumed his charitable works while Winifred basked in the company of cherished friends and relatives.

For the purpose of encouraging 'patients and surgeons alike' in their fight against the disease, a booklet was published by Douglas Guthrie entitled *Forty-Two Years' Survival After Laryngectomy*. It praised John's efforts in that he made a satisfactory recovery, with a 'remarkably good' pharyngeal voice which was 'entirely the result of self-training'. Dr Guthrie also wrote an article on the case in August 1966[64].

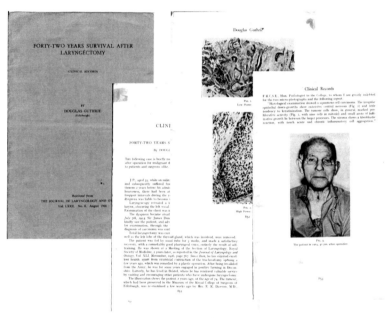

Image 97

This spawned a further rash of press cuttings including, Plymouth Man Had Operation in 1924 - Cancer Case Can End Fears.

In 1967 John won a mild skirmish, as the headline said, 'to have his colds on the national health'. He could neither blew his nose or cough and because

---

[64] Journal of Laryngology & Otology, Volume 80, Issue 08, Aug 1966

he breathed through a hole in his throat he had to wear a special lint square, a bib across the hole which acted as a handkerchief.   The bibs were expensive, £1 for a set of six, and with a cold 'one could easily get through a set in a week', he wrote. So, he took up the matter with the Department of Health saying "you can get falsies, wigs and teeth on the National Health, why not bibs?" They capitulated which was good news for the 200 or so fellow laryngectomees in the Plymouth area and John couldn't wait to tell everyone about his victory, "I wouldn't like people to go on paying when they don't have to".

He was a long term member of the American International Association of Laryngectomees. The IAL News of 1967 in their 'interesting letters from across the sea' section featured a newsy article about John, quoting from his 'gripping' letter which gave a potted history and remarking on the fact that since his operation forty three years earlier he had worn out six silver trachea tubes!

જ્જ્જ

The year 1968 was notably bittersweet. On 16th May the Ministry of Social Security confirmed John's pension at £19/1/4d but wife's allowance was deleted. On 10th July there was the inauguration of the Missing Chords Club in Bristol and John made the pilgrimage from his home in Devon to be with the 45 members.

Then, a frisson of excitement! A large envelope plopped on the doormat which contained an invitation for John to attend 'an Afternoon Party in the Garden of Buckingham Palace' on 23rd July 1968. Of course he would attend and Barbara would be delighted to go in Winifred's place. Barbara went to great pains to find the right hat so she could accompany her father in style, while John stoked up the PR machine. Such news! 'City Pioneer at Palace Party!' In an interview with Barbara Buchanan of the Bristol Evening Post prior to the Garden Party, in which she described John as a straight-backed man who looks no more than 60[65] and 'who has entirely mastered the art of talking without a larynx', Barbara spoke fondly of her dad:

---

[65] He was then aged 80

I grew up in a fantastic world of people, people and more people. Mother and Pop never stopped working, never shut the door. They kept rough records over the years and it really is true that 70,000 servicemen received hospitality, yet there was no committee, no organisation in the normal way. It just seemed to keep going under its own steam.

The article went on to say John was an indefatigable visitor to schools and hospitals or anywhere else, and 'in spite of an operation some think to be disabling, he shows himself to be a 100% Man Alive'. Mrs Buchanan later wrote a private letter to Barbara saying 'only a Scot could do what he's done'. Even with his manner of speech, it was still possible to pick up the Scottish accent. And so proud was John of his Scottish ancestry it would have been quite easy to overlook the fact that he was half English on his father's side! Now, that was something he was uncharacteristically reticent about!

John had read in the Scottish Sunday Post that a second division football team in the Dunfermline Sparks League, Lumphinnans United, desperately needed funds for a new strip. He had been there some 50 years ago and remembered the place with some fondness. Again, never one to miss a PR opportunity, he dashed off a letter to the Chief Inspector of Fife Constabulary enclosing a cheque for two guineas. This produced such a fuss that one would think he handed over several thousands of pounds. The Chief Inspector had brought in a local reporter to make a 'grand story' of the donation and declaring that he was 'over-awed' that an exile living as far as possible away from Lumphinnans could have the kindness to do such a thing. The Secretary of the football club also wrote with his thanks, signing it rather touchingly, 'yours in sport, Mr Robert Sutherland'.

The Garden Party came and went and if that was the zenith, then the nadir was lurking just around the corner.

On the 10th December 1968 Winifred Stevenson Poole collapsed at home and was taken to Greenbank Hospital in Plymouth where, according to her death certificate, she subsequently died of a 'cerebral vascular incident' or stroke. Her funeral took place two days later at Newton Ferrers and John requested no letters, with flowers to go to a local hospice. They had been together for over 47 years, and he was clearly devastated at losing his

all the world and his wife

lifetime companion, the shadow behind his success. He wrote a letter which was published in the News of the World:

> _Old Friend._ _Tens of thousands of service people of all ranks will remember the warm welcome they got at Glen Cottage during the time the RAF Rehabilitation Centre was open._ _Now those thousands who enjoyed the home-made tarts, pies and pastries will be sorry to learn that my wife who did all the cooking has died and been buried in the village churchyard. John Poole, Plymouth, Devon._

One by one, despite the request to the contrary, the sad letters of condolence began rolling in. Winifred was remembered as a 'sweet, kind person' who 'did so much for all of us during the war'. Someone wrote, 'maybe God takes the good ones first ... you were both so kind to all of us when we were children'. 'Happy days that will not be forgotten', somebody else wrote:

> I was one of tens of thousands that was made so welcome in your tiny cottage and enjoyed her delicious pastries. What a lot of work it was for you both, so can I thank you now for what you both did for us and say how grateful we all were.

Barbara became increasingly worried about her father, so she and Witt went down to pick him up to take him to their new home in Solihull, West Midlands, for an extended stay. A curious thing happened as they travelled back along the A30, which was a fast road even in those days. The car shuddered as 'two severe bumps' hit it. Upon investigation they found the culprit - a 10lb rock now lying by the kerbside. The police traced the likely source of this 'exceptional incident' to blasting at nearby Linhay Hill Quarry at Ashburton and said they were very lucky not to have sustained any injury. John kept the rock for many years as some sort of trophy maybe to reinforce his sentiment that life was for living and wasn't he lucky to be alive? No action was taken at the time, but maybe in these more litigious days a civil if not criminal case would have been instituted?

In March 1969, two months after this incident, the DHSS informed John that his service award had been increased by 14/4d to £4/13/8d.

Ever uppermost in his mind was his conviction that not enough was being done in the UK to publicise the plight of the laryngectomee while the IAL and other clubs were burgeoning across America and doing a great job. He would make handwritten notes all over his newsletters, 'Radio, TV and press have all failed. Just what a few of us patients are trying to do'. He was regularly mentioned in the IAL News:

> Mr Poole has a long record of helping his fellow man in time of need, his good deeds going back to WW2.

In one article he was fondly, and somewhat inexplicably, referred to as 'the dour Scot' and another as 'a fiery Scotsman'. In 1970 there was quite an impressive press cutting, 'Cancer Story Started 46 Years Ago' which John immediately sent to Dame Joan Vickers. She thought the article very interesting and wanted to let him know she had taken up the matter he had raised with her and would write as soon as she had received a reply.

Image 98

In 1971 during a coach trip up to the Highlands with Barbara and grandson Donald, he stopped off at Edinburgh to visit Dr Douglas Guthrie who was in frail health. It must have been an emotional time for them as they reminisced about the special bond they had forged nearly fifty years previously. Subsequently Dr Guthrie wrote two further letters that year. One of them thanking him for 'all the trouble' he had taken which presumably meant John's work to publicise the fact that there was a light at the end of the tunnel for those suffering from cancer.

In 1973 John donated his father's forage cap badge or Glengarry to the Scottish United Services Museum at Edinburgh Castle, where it remains on display to this day. To HMS Beagle in Portsmouth he donated a coin commemorating the commissioning of The Beagle and The Adventure in 1827. The Commanding Officer told him it would be mounted in the ship's display cabinet with a card giving origin, details of the ship's commission in the Magellan Straits from 1827 to 1831 and details of who presented it. He was grateful that John had 'bothered' to seek out the 'proper place' for such an historical find.

1974 was notable in that he was guest of honour at the 10th anniversary dinner of Bristol's Missing Chords Club in June.

Image 99

This led to a flurry of press cuttings,[66] one led with: 'John Was Dying of Cancer – 50 Years Ago!'. It mentioned the fact that Dr Douglas Guthrie, also in his eighties, was in hospital, but 'it must be heart-warming' for him to know his old patient, who only had six months to live, is still alive 50 years later! The IAL News also ran the story about the Missing Chords Club which, along with the IAL's Swallow Club of London were all leading voices in stressing the need for rehabilitation services to cancer patients in Great Britain. It stated that Ms Millicent Paintor was a devoted social worker active in the cause of cancer patients' employment problems:

> She shares with Poole and others a strong belief in the necessity for more clubs of laryngectomees in Great Britain.

---

[66] The Sunday Post

To which John scrawled on the bottom: 'Our country has nothing. Even Belgium has clubs'. He certainly had a bee in his bonnet about that.

THE IAL News

PUBLISHED BI-MONTHLY BY THE
INTERNATIONAL ASSOCIATION OF LARYNGECTOMEES
SPONSORED BY THE AMERICAN CANCER SOCIETY

VOLUME XIX • NUMBER 6 • DECEMBER 1974

Fifty years ago there were few survivors from throat cancer, but John I. Poole of Plymouth, England (third from left, seated) is one of them. Now a hale and hearty 88, Poole recently joined with members of the Lost Chord Club of Bristol at a dinner celebrating the group's 10th anniversary. It also marked Poole's 50th year since his operation in Edinburgh, Scotland. The Bristol Club, although unaffiliated, maintains close ties with the IAL's Swallow Club of London. Both clubs are leading voices in stressing the need for rehabilitation services to cancer patients in Great Britain.

Image 100

In 1975 John started up correspondence with Mr J McAuliffe Curtin, an ENT Consultant at the Royal Victoria Eye and Ear Hospital, Dublin.

It was official! To coincide with the official sanction from Guinness World Records that John Iliffe Poole was the longest surviving total laryngectomee patient in the world and the subsequent paragraph in the Guinness Book of Records, the Independent ran a story about The Man Who Beat Cancer – In 1924. It said that he pioneered the 'new voice' technique, using air from the stomach to form sounds, and now used by thousands of people. Stating slightly misleadingly that John was believed to be the 'longest surviving victim of cancer' (which may or may not have been true), the article went on to mention the recent meeting with Dr Douglas Guthrie.

John had refused to think of himself as disabled, it said, and he continued to travel, unsubsidised, to meet people with 'the same affliction'. In the article John commented:

There are 160 Laryngectomy clubs all over the world, most in America, where they do something to raise money. Since my operation, cancer research has discovered this, and that, but they really have discovered nothing. It is still the knife.

But one 'Cancer Specialist' was quick to hit back.

One must admire Mr Poole's courage in the face of this mutilating operation which, incidentally, is not always successful. I feel, however, that I cannot let pass his words 'they have really discovered nothing; it is still the knife'. I fear this statement may give the wrong impression as treatment of larynx cancer using gamma-rays from Telecobalt is an extremely successful method of treatment in the great majority of cases. It has the advantage that the larynx does not have to be removed and that a normal speaking voice is retained which is far superior to the speech of those who have had their larynx removed. Nowadays laryngectomy is usually reserved for those cases who have not responded well to Telecobalt.

'Miracle Man's Message of Hope!' While he was staying with Barbara in Solihull, the Birmingham Evening Mail also reported on John's record-holding status, quoting him:

When I visit people In hospital before and after their operation I tell them that if I can come through the ordeal they can too, especially now there are therapists to help speech development.

Barbara added, 'he gives everyone a great will to live'.

Dr Guthrie died in June 1975.

Image 101

17. KEEPING UP THE PRESSURE

Typical pose - JIP in the late 1960s

In 1976 Barbara and Witt bought an old coaching inn, the Half Moon in Horsington, Somerset and moved there with Virginia and Donald. John had his own annexe (to the left of the picture) and enjoyed being at the hub of a buzzing community once more. Approaching 90, physically active and mentally sharp, he still craved to be busy but in truth, certain jobs had to be 'manufactured' so he would feel that he was earning his keep.

Image 102

He would keep to a strict regime of doing all his own shopping and washing, getting his pension, visiting local hospitals and strengthening his links with Lost Chords.

Apart from all that, his other abiding interests were maintenance of his impressive stamp collection and his garden. Being a practical man, he grew as many vegetables as the small plot would support, and his one concession to any adornment (flowers he considered rather useless) was to grow passion flowers. His impressive and beautiful collection grew on every south-facing wall, fence, trellis and tree.

Image 103

When he wasn't otherwise occupied, letter writing would take over any spare hours he had and he continued to write to anyone about any subject, anything he felt strongly about. "Granddad's at it again", everyone would say as the postman delivered yet more important looking envelopes. One letter he wrote to the local paper is worth quoting:

Stag hunting, fox hunting, digging out badgers and other forms of hunting animals have been brought to the fore recently. Some are cruel sports and have been condemned as such by the cruelty to dumb animals bodies, television and the press. A couple of days ago I noticed fish being weighed to compete in a spearing competition. I am certain fish don't like being speared any more than stags, foxes and other dumb animals don't like being chased by man to be maimed and killed. It is strange to me why one is sport in which cups etc. are presented and the others are regarded as cruel and disgusting. Anyone know why? Dinna Ken[67], Crownhill.

Food still equalled security and thus it loomed large in his everyday regime and he insisted on being self-sufficient. It became a little difficult sharing a busy commercial kitchen with some unusual smelling concoctions that he cooked using mainly leftovers and boiled up every day.

Still reeling from the untimely death of brother Ross in an Irish terrorist bombing, Norris McWhirter still took the time to personally confirm the 1977 printings for the Guinness Book of Records noting that John was now in his 53rd year after the operation. He wrote, 'personally I think that your achievement, which is so inspirational to others, ought to be recognised nationally'. Again, it was not to be.

John sent greetings for the New Year of 1977 to readers of The IAL News, with the fervent wish that 'may a cure be found one day for cancer', but on his copy he hand wrote 'USA and Continent. Great Britain Nothing'. Woodrow Wyatt thanked him for writing to him regarding apartheid.

Rather optimistically John renewed his KOSB Chronicle newsletter subscription for a further ten years, until 1986. Perhaps he believed he would make 98 years, perhaps he thought he was invincible, who knows. In the handwritten confirmation, the Hon Sec at RHQ hoped they would be able to send one to him in his centenary year. John was believed to be one of the oldest, if not the oldest living Borderer at that time, and the Hon Sec

---

[67] From the Scottish: 'I don't know' - a pseudonym JIP used to use.

a cat's lick and a promise

requested a note of John's service, date of joining, places visited and a photo, if it wasn't 'too much to ask'. Presumably John wasn't slow to comply.

The Newsletter of the Lost Chord Club of New South Wales that year remarked, 'we think this youngster will make a good publicity officer for our club in Britain'. Frenchay Hospital made a tape recording of his voice which they thought would be a great encouragement to others.

There followed a succession of letters to a number of prominent ENT hospitals throughout the United Kingdom. John had sent each one a sheaf of Laryngectomy emergency/patient warning cards which presumably gave details of medical history and contact points. It could just be possible that he had helped to devised them and their prime function was to highlight the fact that the wearer was a neck-breather and would need special attention. Amongst others, the Royal Victoria Hospital, Belfast, Queen Elizabeth Hospital, Edgbaston, Children's ENT, Cardiff, Newcastle General, Royal Victoria, Dublin, even the British Red Cross all thanked him.

Mr McKinlay FRCSEd[68] wrote from Glasgow stating he had passed round John's letter to all his ENT colleagues in the Western District of Glasgow. He had known Dr Douglas Guthrie very well, also Sir James Dundas-Grant who was 'well known for his work on hearing and deafness just after the 1st WW'. He added:

Speech Therapy nowadays is a very highly organised medical auxiliary subject with very highly trained ladies – teaching of 'oesophagal' speech now devolves on them. I would be interested to know how you in 1924 were guided in your attempts to regain speech.

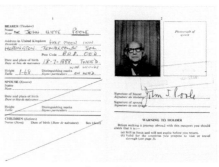

Image 104

The letter ended by wishing John 'all the best at Marseilles'. On 27 April 1978 at the age of 90, he became the proud possessor of a British

---

68 Formerly of Royal Victoria Hospital, Dublin

Visitor's Passport: Born 18.7.1888.   Tweed.   Distinguishing marks – war wounds on head.

He was now ready for the last adventure of his life, a trip to the 10th World Congress of Laryngectomees in Marseilles from 27th to 30th June 1978.

**DEUXIEME CONGRES MONDIAL DES LARYNGECTOMISES
MARSEILLE - FRANCE 27 - 30 JUIN 1978**

Image 105

By all accounts, and from the photos he left, he had a great time as he was, quite rightly, at the hub of all the activity that he had been working towards and holding dear for over half a century.   Rising to take a bow at this important meeting and being acknowledged by his peers and learned medical staff alike, it was a crowning glory for him and he must have felt it was well worth his while to have fought and never given up. Inspirational he certainly was, especially for people who found themselves struggling to survive in the mundanity that is so often all we know as life.

After 31 years, Barbara and Witt parted and John did his best to comfort her, although he was not a great one for emotionality. Witt wrote a sad letter at the time to try and explain to the old man but John would have seen things differently.

Dear Pop, I was very moved by your kind birthday card and thank you very much. Maybe I felt I could never face you again after the unhappy upset between Barbara and me. She is she and I am myself and lately we have seemed to clash and realised that we were happier apart. It's all very sad, but good comes out of bad and things do happen for the best in some way sometimes. My wish is that she will find future happiness in her life. I shall always keep faith to make sure that she is not left stranded, but like you my needs are small. Hope you are keeping well and long may yer lumb reek[69]! Aye, Witt

In John's day, you married for life. He certainly did, and he was the first to recognise that his marriage had not been smooth. So, at the age of 91, although he was flexible of brain and always embracing new ideas and technologies, his views on morality were rather entrenched and sadly he was never able to fully understand their situation.

John would have preferred practical ways of helping Barbara, like the time she got a thrombosis in her leg and at the age of 73 he walked mile upon mile, 6 or 7 miles, every day with her as he knew she was under doctor's orders to keep the leg moving. Like the countless times he gave her advice on budgeting and household management, and he was always there for her.

Image 106

John's 90th birthday in July 1978 was a joyful occasion. Flushed with emotion and good health, he greeted all the guests to his birthday party. The huge fires at each end of the ancient, beamed lounge bar of the Half Moon crackled, the tables were laden with food and he had a wonderful time; everyone did. Barbara had secretly arranged for an ex Pipe Major, Leslie de Laspee to play the bagpipes. In Autumn 1978 Mr de Laspee wrote a letter to the KOSB Chronicle describing the event:

---

[69] You keep on breathing; lit. 'your lung breathe'

All went well at Tony Poole's birthday party on July 18th. I did not know this Tony Poole - he served before my time, but it is his brother, who also seems to have had the nickname of Tony whom I knew. He was in India and China with me, but is now dead. This Tony lives with his daughter who has a lovely old world pub (the Half Moon). He is in remarkably good health for the age of 91.

Many members of the village congregated at the pub for his birthday celebrations as he seemed a very well liked person. At the appropriate time I piped in a birthday cake, but as soon as he saw my cap badge he ignored the cake completely and almost broke down. He was delighted to see the Royal Stuart tartan and the rest of the evening was spent in talking of the Regiment and my playing the old tunes that he remembered. Luckily, quite a few of his serving comrades I just about remembered too.

Image 107

It might be of interest to you that he is in the Guinness Book of Records as the first man to have a cancer operation on the throat in 1925, just after he left the Regiment.

During the mid to late 1970s the Post-it was invented, as was the disposable razor and the catalytic converter. The rings around Uranus were discovered, Viking 1 landed on Mars, the Russian Soyuz 19 docked with Apollo 18. The game of Space Invaders became all the rage and following a 'sci-fi' theme, the films Superman and Star Wars were both released. IBM launched the laser printer, Apple computers were founded and the Apple II became the first mass produced home computer. The Sony Walkman was introduced, as was the first automatic focus camera. There was a nuclear accident in Pennsylvania. The iconic Mother Teresa was awarded the Nobel prize and the Polish Pope with the common touch, Karol Wojtyla became John Paul 11. South Vietnam surrendered to North Vietnam in 1975 while four years later Russia invaded Afghanistan.

18. THE LAST POST

JIP's last resting place, Holy Cross Church, Newton Ferrers

Well into his 91st year John still continued with his weekly regime. He would appear at grand-daughter Lynda's house two doors from the Half Moon ready for his regular lift into the town. Hat, blazer (with KOSB badge) and raincoat on, shoes polished, come rain or shine he would be there half an hour or forty-five minutes before the pre-arranged time, tapping on the front door. Whereupon he would wait, feet tapping intermittently, until she appeared at the front door.

Image 108

John began corresponding with an ENT specialist in Cedar Falls, Iowa, USA who reminisced about Douglas Guthrie and his pioneering work.

At the end of the year came a letter from Annie Howe, widow of a freeman of Berwick-Upon-Tweed:

> Dear Toney[70], glad to know that you are still in the land of the living. I'm sure I remember your father. Willie and I were keen supporters of the old KOSB. Once a Borderer, always a Borderer. Alas the old KOSB barracks are now empty. I remember my mother taking me on the Sunday afternoons after the Boer War to visit wounded KOSB who had been customers of the Pilot Inn. I have fond memories of the mugs of tea arriving for the patients and I had to take a sip out of each mug. Memories? I live on my memories although I am now in my 84th year.

---

[70] She always called him Toney

Up the Borderers! With love to you and yours from Annie Howe who was born in the Pilot Inn, Low Greens in 1895.

She must have seemed a mere youngster! It was Annie who sent him details regarding the freemen of Berwick, a tradition dating from the time of King James 1st who gave a parcel of land in 1603 to 66 gentlemen (of 52 families). In early 1979 she wrote, 'there's only 73 of us now'. And it was Annie who would send John his last letter just a few months later.

He loved all his family but was particularly fond of Daphne, the Half Moon's cook, and decided to make her a gift of 5 yards of Leslie tartan although it's not clear what she did with it. Scotsmen and Regiments take these things very seriously indeed and the other tartan he was entitled to wear was the Montrose Graham. The Leslie tartan (antique) on the left, below, was the one worn by the Earl of Leven back in the 17th century and adopted by his regiment the King's Borderers to wear on the cap badges and trews. The Montrose Graham tartan, on the right here, was his family one.

Image 109

John had a letter from his sister Eva Holdsworth, living at Wood Lane, Rothwell, Leeds. She mentioned that she had passed his Christmas card on to 'May' – could that have been another sister? Mr McAuliffe Curtin, FRCSI, FACS wrote from Dublin wishing John 'every success for the coming year'. This was followed by some terrible news when Muriel Chiswell, a lifetime friend from Newton Ferrers, wrote that their best friend Ivy Pengelly (Auntie Ivy) had died. It seemed that life was finally closing in on him.

There were still lighter moments, though. John and Barbara had a visit from a gentleman called George Doughty, a laryngectomee from Tasmania's Lost Chords Club. One of the highlights of his trip to England had been to stay at Barbara's inn, the Half Moon, an 'old English country inn with its beams, copper ware etc'. He had been a bit confused over the words 'free house' over the door until it was explained to him. By all accounts he and John got on like a house on fire.

৩৽৩৽৩৽

Then there was a dramatic decline in John's usually robust health, so much so that it was one of the few times in his life he had to take to his bed. He was later moved to Wincanton's little cottage hospital where he died barely two weeks later. He seemed to have a light, an aura about him that few would ever have thought could be extinguished. It was a shock to find how icy cold his forehead was.

On the 23rd June 1979 John Iliffe Poole was laid to rest next to Winifred in the tiny village cemetery of the Church of the Holy Cross overlooking the sparkling River Yealm in their beloved Newton Ferrers.

John had always taken great interest in advancements in medical science and following his own operation in 1924 time hardly seemed to have stood still. Awe-inspiring developments had taken place such as Alexander Fleming discovering penicillin, the invention of the electron microscope. Nuclear energy was well and truly on its way following the successful splitting of an atom, James Chadwick discovered the neutron and there was the first controlled nuclear chain reaction at the University of Chicago plus the first nuclear reactor.

The first sex change operation was carried out in 1950 and as early as 1957 James Watson and his team discovered the structure of DNA. In 1967 while DNA was being synthesised in a test tube, Dr Christiaan Barnard pioneered the first heart transplant. In 1968 the epidural anaesthetic was devised, the first test tube fertilisation of a human egg took place in 1969, leading to Louise Brown's birth in 1978. Links between heart disease and a high fat diet were discovered, as was one between lung cancer and smoking. Silicone breast implants were introduced, the hearing aid launched, freeze drying was discovered and the hallucinogenic properties of LSD established.

SOFT WORDS BUTTER NO PARSNIPS

And in the years immediately following John's death, there were more significant medical breakthroughs. There was first artificial heart operation and the first operation was performed on an unborn foetus, genetic fingerprinting was discovered using DNA, lasers began to be used in surgery, liposuction was offered in Europe for the first time, the HIV virus identified. The first damages were awarded for illness caused by passive smoking, the WHO[71] declared the end of smallpox, the Human Genome Project was launched in San Diego and NASA scientists announced they had found proof of living organisms on a Mars meteorite.

Indeed, as you read this book, more and more exciting things are happening virtually every day with major inroads being made around the world into disease and illness following years of committed research by scores of dedicated people. Since his landmark operation in those bleak years following the war, John devoted the remainder of his life to publicising cancer in all its many forms. People had a habit of referring to it as 'the big C' just as though if they actually said its name they would invoke it, the same as in 'the olden days' when people talked about the devil; they rarely spoke his name, preferring to call him 'old Nick' or 'Grim' etc.

John's optimism and rude good health bore testament to the fact that the word cancer was not synonymous with death, it was just an obstacle to overcome. After all, he did it. His papers are spattered with references to his fervent wish that they would soon find a cure for cancer but sadly it was not to happen in his lifetime. If he was here now, he would be muttering:

Well, they have found ways of putting men on the moon; making a sheep[72]; sending letters across the world in seconds, transplanting a face; photographing energy waves[73], why cannot they find a simple cure for cancer?

Most of us love happy endings, and, literally as the finishing touches are put to this little book, news has come of potentially the most spectacular breakthrough ever in the fight against cancer! Scientists have just successfully completed mapping the human genome and are confident that in only a few years they will have fully mapped all cancer genes. If all goes to plan there is

---

[71] World Health Organisation
[72] Dolly the sheep was cloned in 1991
[73] Kirlian photography

a real possibility that cancer will become but a dim memory for future generations. How wonderful is that?

❧❧❧

Before she died on 23rd November 2003, Barbara was able to supply the missing link regarding the circumstances of her brother Donald's death. She was so excited at this book being written, she was eighty, increasingly infirm and over the years it had never seemed right to probe too deeply, especially if it could have caused her sadness. Like her parents, she would never really talk about Donald but fortunately she ready to explain that what actually happened to Donald was far more upsetting than the more sanitised version given to them at the time, but they were not to find this out until some months later, just after the war finally ended.

One of Donald's comrade-in-arms from his regiment, The King's Company, The Grenadiers, made his way to Glen Cot because he felt it his duty to explain what really happened. It seems that Donald had been wounded, the friend saw him picked up on a stretcher and moved to the ambulance lorry and the friend watched in horror as the wounded man was machine-gunned while still on the stretcher resting on the tailgate of the vehicle.

❧❧❧

The last dated letter in John's bulging files was one from Annie Howe dated 6th March 1979. At the end of it, she wrote:

> Here's to the thistle that grows all around, the cross and the crown. Here's to the lion – who everybody knows is the pride of its country and a terror to its foes.

List of Images